Alcohol

OPPOSING VIEWPOINTS®

Karen F. Balkin, *Book Editor*

Daniel Leone, *President*
Bonnie Szumski, *Publisher*
Scott Barbour, *Managing Editor*
Helen Cothran, *Senior Editor*

OPPOSING
VIEWPOINTS®
SERIES

GREENHAVEN
PRESS®

THOMSON
————*————
GALE

San Diego • Detroit • New York • San Francisco • Cleveland
New Haven, Conn. • Waterville, Maine • London • Munich

THOMSON

GALE

© 2004 by Greenhaven Press. Greenhaven Press is an imprint of The Gale Group, Inc., a division of Thomson Learning, Inc.

Greenhaven® and Thomson Learning™ are trademarks used herein under license.

For more information, contact
Greenhaven Press
27500 Drake Rd.
Farmington Hills, MI 48331-3535
Or you can visit our Internet site at http://www.gale.com

LIBRARY OF CONGRESS CATALOGING-IN-PUBLICATION DATA

Alcohol: opposing viewpoints / Karen F. Balkin, book editor.
   p. cm. — (Opposing viewpoints series)
  Includes bibliographical references and index.
  ISBN 0-7377-1216-3 (lib. bdg. : alk. paper) —
  ISBN 0-7377-1215-5 (pbk. : alk. paper)
    1. Alcoholism. 2. Drinking of alcoholic beverages—Health aspects
3. Alcoholics—Rehabilitation. 4. Alcoholism—Prevention. I. Balkin, Karen F.,
1949– . II. Opposing viewpoints series (Unnumbered)
HV5035.A459 2004
362.292—dc22   2003049297

Printed in the United States of America

DEC - - 2003

"Congress shall make
no law...abridging the
freedom of speech, or of
the press."

First Amendment to the U.S. Constitution

The basic foundation of our democracy is the First
Amendment guarantee of freedom of expression.
The Opposing Viewpoints Series is dedicated to the
concept of this basic freedom and the idea that it is
more important to practice it than to enshrine it.

Contents

Why Consider Opposing Viewpoints?

"The only way in which a human being can make some approach to knowing the whole of a subject is by hearing what can be said about it by persons of every variety of opinion and studying all modes in which it can be looked at by every character of mind. No wise man ever acquired his wisdom in any mode but this."

John Stuart Mill

In our media-intensive culture it is not difficult to find differing opinions. Thousands of newspapers and magazines and dozens of radio and television talk shows resound with differing points of view. The difficulty lies in deciding which opinion to agree with and which "experts" seem the most credible. The more inundated we become with differing opinions and claims, the more essential it is to hone critical reading and thinking skills to evaluate these ideas. Opposing Viewpoints books address this problem directly by presenting stimulating debates that can be used to enhance and teach these skills. The varied opinions contained in each book examine many different aspects of a single issue. While examining these conveniently edited opposing views, readers can develop critical thinking skills such as the ability to compare and contrast authors' credibility, facts, argumentation styles, use of persuasive techniques, and other stylistic tools. In short, the Opposing Viewpoints Series is an ideal way to attain the higher-level thinking and reading skills so essential in a culture of diverse and contradictory opinions.

In addition to providing a tool for critical thinking, Opposing Viewpoints books challenge readers to question their own strongly held opinions and assumptions. Most people form their opinions on the basis of upbringing, peer pressure, and personal, cultural, or professional bias. By reading carefully balanced opposing views, readers must directly confront new ideas as well as the opinions of those with whom they disagree. This is not to simplistically argue that

everyone who reads opposing views will—or should—
change his or her opinion. Instead, the series enhances readers' understanding of their own views by encouraging con-
frontation with opposing ideas. Careful examination of others' views can lead to the readers' understanding of the
logical inconsistencies in their own opinions, perspective on
why they hold an opinion, and the consideration of the possibility that their opinion requires further evaluation.

Evaluating Other Opinions

To ensure that this type of examination occurs, Opposing
Viewpoints books present all types of opinions. Prominent
spokespeople on different sides of each issue as well as well-
known professionals from many disciplines challenge the
reader. An additional goal of the series is to provide a forum
for other, less known, or even unpopular viewpoints. The
opinion of an ordinary person who has had to make the decision to cut off life support from a terminally ill relative, for
example, may be just as valuable and provide just as much insight as a medical ethicist's professional opinion. The editors
have two additional purposes in including these less known
views. One, the editors encourage readers to respect others'
opinions—even when not enhanced by professional credibility. It is only by reading or listening to and objectively evaluating others' ideas that one can determine whether they are
worthy of consideration. Two, the inclusion of such viewpoints encourages the important critical thinking skill of objectively evaluating an author's credentials and bias. This
evaluation will illuminate an author's reasons for taking a
particular stance on an issue and will aid in readers' evaluation of the author's ideas.

It is our hope that these books will give readers a deeper
understanding of the issues debated and an appreciation of
the complexity of even seemingly simple issues when good
and honest people disagree. This awareness is particularly
important in a democratic society such as ours in which
people enter into public debate to determine the common
good. Those with whom one disagrees should not be re-
garded as enemies but rather as people whose views deserve
careful examination and may shed light on one's own.

Thomas Jefferson once said that "difference of opinion leads to inquiry, and inquiry to truth." Jefferson, a broadly educated man, argued that "if a nation expects to be ignorant and free . . . it expects what never was and never will be." As individuals and as a nation, it is imperative that we consider the opinions of others and examine them with skill and discernment. The Opposing Viewpoints Series is intended to help readers achieve this goal.

David L. Bender and Bruno Leone,
Founders

Greenhaven Press anthologies primarily consist of previously published material taken from a variety of sources, including periodicals, books, scholarly journals, newspapers, government documents, and position papers from private and public organizations. These original sources are often edited for length and to ensure their accessibility for a young adult audience. The anthology editors also change the original titles of these works in order to clearly present the main thesis of each viewpoint and to explicitly indicate the opinion presented in the viewpoint. These alterations are made in consideration of both the reading and comprehension levels of a young adult audience. Every effort is made to ensure that Greenhaven Press accurately reflects the original intent of the authors included in this anthology.

Introduction

"Unfortunately, many women continue to drink during pregnancy. Furthermore, many of the women who continue to drink during pregnancy are at highest risk for having children with fetal alcohol syndrome and related problems. Thus, finding potent new ways to reach populations at risk and to influence changes in their behavior remains a challenge for alcohol research."

—*Enoch Gordis, director of the National Institute for Alcohol Abuse and Alcoholism*

"I am adopted and my mom died so no one will ever know when or how much or how often my mom drank. I just know I have to live with it," Liz Kulp said in *The Best I Can Be: Living with Fetal Alcohol Syndrome or Effects. The Best I Can Be*, a book written by her adopted mother Jodee Kulp, details Liz's struggle against the brain and metabolic damage she suffered as the result of her birth mother's drinking. According to the National Organization of Fetal Alcohol Syndrome (NOFAS), in the United States as many as twelve thousand infants are born each year with Fetal Alcohol Syndrome (FAS), a set of physical, mental, and neurobehavioral birth defects characterized by facial abnormalities and growth retardation. Three times as many babies have Alcohol-Related Neurodevelopment Disorder (ARND)—functional or mental impairment without facial abnormalities or growth problems—or Alcohol-Related Birth Defects (ARBD), which include malformations in the skeletal and major organ systems. Experts from NOFAS argue that FAS/ARND/ARBD affect more newborns every year than Down syndrome, cystic fibrosis, spina bifida, and sudden infant death syndrome combined. Together, FAS/ARND/ARBD comprise the leading known cause of mental retardation in the United States and affect every racial and ethnic group. These alcohol-caused syndromes present stark evidence of the devastation alcohol can cause and point to some of the medical and legal issues surrounding alcohol use.

People born with FAS/ARND/ARBD will spend their lives trying to overcome various difficulties in visual, auditory, language, and tactile processing. Like Liz, they will always have fine and gross motor skill problems and face challenges in their social and behavioral development. For example, Liz struggles daily with language because parts of her brain that process sounds into words and words into language were damaged by alcohol before she was born. The hugs and snuggles most children cherish were repugnant to Liz as an infant and young child—alcohol-caused brain damage retarded her ability to process tactile sensations. She was almost ten years old before she really enjoyed a hug.

The economic and emotional costs to individuals suffering from FAS/ARND/ARBD and their families is obvious, but the syndromes' costs to society are incalculable as well. The Office of National Drug Control Policy estimates the 1992 cost to U.S. taxpayers for medical and specialized care for children born with FAS/ARND/ARBD was $1.9 billion. Many of these children will require a lifetime of custodial care. Ironically, while devastatingly irreversible, the damage done to a fetus by alcohol is totally preventable. Jodee Kulp notes that FAS "is 100 percent preventable and our number one cause of birth defects, yet as a culture we ignore it."

Scientists have known for many years that alcohol is a teratogen, a substance known to be harmful to human development. When a pregnant woman drinks, alcohol enters her bloodstream and then goes through blood vessels in the placenta to her growing baby's blood supply. Alcohol use can interfere with healthy development of the fetus and cause FAS/ARND/ARBD. Some scientists argue that it is not so much the total amount of alcohol consumed over time but rather a high number of drinks consumed at one time— binge drinking—that puts the fetus at greatest risk. Since there is no known safe amount of alcohol that can be imbibed during pregnancy, the simplest method of preventing FAS/ARND/ARBD is for women to avoid alcohol completely during all phases of pregnancy. In fact, that is what most doctors recommend. Enoch Gordis, director of the National Institute for Alcohol Abuse and Alcoholism contends, "Until such safe dose, if it exists, can be determined, the only responsible advice to women who wish to become pregnant and to those who are pregnant is to avoid alcohol use entirely."

The Department of Health and Human Services has long recognized that alcohol-caused fetal injuries are a serious public health problem. Since 1981 the surgeon general has recommended abstinence during pregnancy and required that all alcoholic beverages be clearly labeled with a warning outlining the risk of alcohol to fetal development. Establishments selling alcoholic beverages are required to post the same message on signs in plain view. Moreover, the federal government provides prenatal programs, public service announcements, health articles, and brochures advising abstinence during pregnancy. State and local agencies, as well, fund programs that target specific groups known to be at higher risk than the general population, such as women who reside in communities with heavy per capita alcohol use.

However, results of a study published in the January 2003 issue of the journal *Alcoholism: Clinical and Experimental Research*, indicate that many women continue to drink throughout their pregnancies even though they have been advised of the danger. One of the researchers who conducted the study, Heather A. Flynn of the University of Michigan Medical School, concluded, "Despite increasing public awareness of the harmful effects of drinking during pregnancy, many women consume alcohol in varying degrees while pregnant."

There is no cure for FAS/ARND/ARBD—prevention through abstinence and early identification of affected individuals offer the most viable solutions for this horrific alcohol-caused problem. The younger that children can be diagnosed (Liz Kulp was twelve-and-a-half before her FAS diagnosis was confirmed) and offered social support, special education, behavioral and cognitive therapy, and appropriate medication, the greater their chances of ultimately functioning at a higher level. Jodee Kulp concludes, "[Liz and I] believe that we can make a significant impact on society if we help persons with FAS become the best they can be . . . our prison system, homeless shelters and institutions should not be the structured environment they live their adult lives in."

The potential for prenatal injury is just one of the complex problems surrounding the use of alcohol in American society. Authors in *Alcohol: Opposing Viewpoints* explore other alcohol-related issues in the following chapters: Is Alcohol Use Beneficial to Human Health? What Are the Causes of Alcohol Abuse? How Should Alcoholism Be Treated? What Measures Should Be Taken to Reduce Alcohol-Related Problems? While recent scientific discoveries have added to the layperson's knowledge about alcohol and its effect on the human body, no one has yet resolved the many medical and legal issues surrounding this ancient beverage.

CHAPTER 1

Is Alcohol Use Beneficial to Human Health?

Chapter Preface

High-fat cheeses, cream soups and sauces, desserts rich with eggs, butter, and cream. These are just a few of the foods that make the French diet high in saturated fat and extremely cholesterol-rich. Yet, according to research first presented in the early 1990s by Serge Renaud, a scientist at INSERM, the national medical research center in Lyon, France, French people have one of the lowest levels of coronary heart disease (CHD) in the Western world. This is the French Paradox—a high-cholesterol diet known to cause CHD eaten by a population that exhibits very low CHD levels. The explanation for this apparent contradiction is that the wine French people consume has a beneficial effect on their cardiovascular systems. Drinking moderate amounts of alcohol daily, as most French people do, helps prevent damage to their arteries caused by a high-cholesterol diet and thus lowers their risk of CHD. Renaud explains: "Growing up around Bordeaux [a region in France known for its wine], you know instinctively that wine is good for you. My grandparents, their friends, all lived to be 80 or 90. I knew there was some special reason."

Renaud's research became well-known in this country in 1991 when the CBS news magazine, *60 Minutes*, interviewed him. Four years later in 1995, *60 Minutes* aired a follow-up report on continuing research into the beneficial effects of alcohol. U.S. physician and French Paradox researcher R. Curtis Ellison, chief of Preventive Medicine and Epidemiology at Boston University School of Medicine, was interviewed on the show and commented that Renaud's research had clear implications for America:

> Moderate alcohol consumption, especially moderate red wine consumption, is associated with much lower risk of heart disease and stroke, leading causes of death in the United States. . . . I think the data are now so convincing that the total mortality rates are lower among moderate drinkers. It seems quite clear that we should not do anything that would decrease moderate drinkers in the population.

The 1995 Copenhagen Heart Study, conducted by researchers at the Copenhagen University Institute for Preventive Medicine, supported Renaud's and Ellison's conclusions regarding the French Paradox. However, Danish researchers emphasized that the benefits of alcohol were dependent on the European pattern of daily mealtime consumption and that the American pattern of binge drinking had a detrimental effect on health. According to Morten Gronbaek, a scientist at Copenhagen University, "our study shows that light and moderate wine drinking, in contrast with beer and spirits drinking, is associated with a strong dose-dependent decrease in all-cause mortality, attributable to a decrease in mortality from cardiovascular and cerebrovascular disease as well as from other causes." Most scientists attribute the healthful properties of wine—especially red wine—to its high concentration of antioxidants called polyphenols. Polyphenols prevent the buildup of fatty lesions that can block arteries and cause CHD.

Many scientists, however, challenge the validity of the French Paradox. According to French researcher Pierre Ducimetiere, "Coronary incidence data now deny there is a French Paradox." Ducimetiere claims that studies purporting to demonstrate the protective effect of wine utilize flawed methods of data collection. The so-called French Paradox, he argues "is a consequence of different ways of coding coronary mortality." Nutrition experts also doubt the French Paradox but for a different reason. They maintain that it is the French diet overall, not just wine, that contributes to a low incidence of CHD. While they acknowledge the high percentage of unhealthy high-cholesterol animal fats that most French people eat, they claim that the typical French diet also contains substantial amounts of healthful olive oil, as well as fresh fruits and vegetables that provide fiber, B vitamins, and antioxidants that help protect the heart. Moreover, many experts point to the relaxed, stress-free mealtimes enjoyed by French people as another reason for less CHD.

The debate over the French Paradox is just one example of the arguments surrounding the complex question of whether the use of alcohol is beneficial to human health. Authors in the following chapter seek to answer this important social and medical question.

"A pattern of regular consumption at least three to four days per week is associated with the lowest risk of heart attacks."

Frequent, Moderate Drinking Benefits Human Health

Harvard School of Public Health

According to a recent study, frequent, moderate consumption of alcoholic beverages offers significant cardiovascular benefits, coauthors of the study argue in the following viewpoint. Men who drank one serving of an alcoholic beverage at least three times a week experienced the greatest reduction in risk of coronary disease. Further, the coauthors contend that alcohol's influence on the body is short-lived. Thus, infrequent drinking, while still beneficial, does not offer the greatest protection. The coauthors are from the Harvard School of Public Health, which is research-based and advances the public's health through learning, discovery, and communication.

As you read, consider the following questions:
1. According to the editors, how long did the Harvard School of Public Health (HSPH) study last?
2. What four features of alcohol use did the HSPH study assess?
3. In addition to raising the level of HDL, what is alcohol's impact on the body, in the editors' opinion?

Harvard School of Public Health, "Study Finds Frequent Consumption of Alcohol Linked to Lower Risk of Heart Attack in Men," www.hsph.harvard.edu, January 8, 2003. Copyright © 2003 by Harvard School of Public Health. Reproduced by permission of Beth Israel Deaconess Medical Center and Harvard School of Public Health.

Daily or near-daily servings of beer, wine or spirits may help protect men from heart attacks, according to the results of a large, long-term study by researchers at Beth Israel Deaconess Medical Center (BIDMC) and the Harvard School of Public Health (HSPH). The findings, which appear in the Jan. 9 [2003] issue of *The New England Journal of Medicine*, show that men who drank moderate amounts of alcoholic beverages three or more times a week had a risk of myocardial infarction 30 to 35 percent lower than nondrinkers.

The observational study, which tracked the drinking habits of nearly 40,000 men over a 12-year period, provides an important clue as to how alcohol helps guard against coronary heart disease, and for the first time, strongly suggests that routine consumption of alcoholic beverages is key.

"Even relatively modest amounts of alcohol may be protective if consumed frequently," said the study's first author, Kenneth Mukamal, MD, MPH, of BIDMC's Division of General Medicine and Primary Care and Assistant Professor of Medicine at Harvard Medical School. "Our results document that a pattern of regular consumption at least three to four days per week is associated with the lowest risk of heart attacks."

The researchers analyzed data from the Health Professionals Follow-up Study based at HSPH. Subjects included a total of 38,077 male health professionals between the ages of 40 and 75. Beginning in 1986, the subject responded to a detailed questionnaire regarding diet, medical history and patterns of alcohol consumption. They then completed follow-up questionnaires every four years thereafter until 1998.

The researchers assessed four features of alcohol use: type of alcohol consumed (beer, liquor, red wine or white wine); the average amount of alcohol consumed; whether or not the beverage was consumed with a meal; and the number of days per week that alcohol was consumed. The authors documented 1,418 cases of both fatal and nonfatal myocardial infarction among the study participants during the 12-year period.

Moderate, Frequent Drinking Offered the Most Protection

After adjusting for a number of factors—age, smoking, physical activity, parental history of heart disease, body-mass index, diabetes, high blood pressure, high cholesterol levels, aspirin use and diet—the findings showed that alcohol consumption was associated with a lower risk of coronary heart disease, regardless of the type of beverage, the quantity consumed per drinking day, whether or not it was consumed with meals or the type of coronary outcome. The variable that was consistently associated with the lowest risk was the number of times per week a participant drank alcoholic beverages.

Alcohol and Brain Function

Alcohol may not only be good for the heart. The noggin may benefit as well.

A study conducted by Dr. Guiseppe Zuccala of the Catholic University of the Sacred Heart in Rome found that moderate alcohol use may protect the brain from mental decline associated with aging. In the report published in the December 2001 issue of *Alcoholism: Clinical & Experimental Research*, Dr. Zuccala studied the mental abilities and alcohol use of nearly 16,000 Italian men and women over the age of 65: approximately 8,700 regular drinkers, and 7,000 non-drinkers. Moderate use of alcohol was associated with a 40 percent lower risk of mental impairment. Dr. Zuccala postulated that the reasons for the difference may be alcohol's beneficial effects on blood pressure and blood flow or perhaps the slowing of arterial disease.

Greg Glaser, *All About Beer*, July 2002.

After separating study subjects into categories based on whether they drank no alcoholic beverages, drank fewer than once or twice a week, drank three to four times a week, or drank five to seven times a week, the researchers found that the subjects in the categories of three-to-four or five-to-seven drinks per week had a 32 to 37 percent reduced risk of coronary heart disease, compared with abstainers.

The reasons behind these findings may be twofold, noted Mukamal. "In general, alcohol raises levels of HDL, the good cholesterol. But, in addition alcohol impacts the body's sensitivity to insulin, as well as platelet function and clotting factors." Through these additional effects, he said, alcohol may be improving how the body metabolizes blood sugar and helping to prevent the development of blood clots, which can lead to a heart attack.

"It seems that alcohol's influence on platelets and clotting is relatively short term," he added. "This could explain why frequent alcohol intake is of greatest benefit in helping to guard against coronary heart disease."

Eric Rimm, ScD, Associate Professor of Nutrition and Epidemiology at the Harvard School of Public Health and the study's senior author, added that this was one of the first studies to document a lower risk of heart attacks among men who increase their alcohol consumption over time. Study subjects who increased consumption by one drink per day during the 12 years of the study had a 22 percent lower risk of heart attack than men whose consumption patterns remained unchanged.

Mukamal cautioned that these findings cannot be generalized without reservation. "It's always tricky to offer individual advice based on observational studies of large numbers of people," he noted. "You need to take into account other considerations—for example, a person's family history, the risk of driving in an impaired state, the risk of developing liver problems—before deciding on the safest level of alcohol consumption for that individual. However, among men who drink alcohol, consuming one or two drinks a day three or more times a week may help reduce the risk of coronary heart disease."

"We found no protective effect of moderate alcohol for coronary heart disease"

The Health Benefits of Frequent, Moderate Drinking Are Exaggerated

George Davey-Smith, interviewed by Natasha Mitchell

George Davey-Smith is a professor of epidemiology at the University of Bristol in the United Kingdom. In the following viewpoint, taken from an interview he did with medical reporter Natasha Mitchell for Radio National in Australia, Davey-Smith argues that the moderate use of alcohol has not been proven to have cardiovascular benefits. Further, a study he conducted in Scotland concluded that binge drinking, not frequent moderate drinking, was more typical of average drinkers and was harmful to the cardiovascular system. Davey-Smith is leery of advising people to drink moderately; such advice will likely encourage both moderate and binge drinkers to drink more, to the detriment of their health. Radio National is Australia's only national noncommercial radio broadcaster.

As you read, consider the following questions:

1. According to Davey-Smith's research, which coronary problem shows a strong positive association with drinking alcohol?
2. How will the promotion of drinking as a healthy choice affect moderate and heavy drinkers, in Davey-Smith's opinion?

*N*atasha Mitchell: Welcome. . . .
  [July 1999] saw the launch of Scotland's brand, spanking new parliament. But for those Scots who spent the weekend throwing back the pints, hoping a drink is good for their health, they may have been misguided, according to a large study of Scottish men.

To that age old debate, it's been reported over recent years that drinking moderate amounts of alcohol in fact protects you against coronary heart disease. More so than not drinking at all.

But results just in quell this popular orthodoxy. Professor George Davey-Smith, from the University of Bristol.

George Davey-Smith: The popular view is that drinking is good for the heart. The idea is that moderate alcohol consumption reduces heart disease. Some previous studies have been interpreted as suggesting that drinking might even protect against stroke; that's the quite popularly disseminated view. And our study suggested that there was no protective effect on heart disease, and most importantly, there was quite a strong positive association between drinking alcohol and stroke.

Drinking Increases the Risk of Stroke

How did differing amounts of alcohol affect the men's health differently?

Well what we found with stroke was just the more you drank the higher your risk of stroke. And then we looked at alcohol-related causes of death, ones which we just know are very strongly alcohol-related, like cirrhosis, like dying through acts of violence, like oesophageal cancer, and those alcohol-related causes of death unsurprisingly, were very strongly related to drinking indeed. We found no protective effect of moderate alcohol for coronary heart disease. When we just looked at the straightforward data, the men who drank most had the highest rates of coronary heart disease. When we took into account that those men also smoked more and tended to come from worse social circumstances, that elevation in coronary heart disease risk was largely explained by other behavioural factors and social factors. So overall, we think there is little association between alcohol and coronary heart disease, but certainly it wasn't protective; we showed

22

no strong protective effect of alcohol.

This study started more than 20 years ago, and took some 6,000 men aged 36 to 64 from workplaces in the West of Scotland.

The men's alcohol intake was monitored, along with risk factors for heart disease, like high blood pressure and cholesterol.

Professor Davey-Smith thinks it's the fact that they looked at ordinary people with ordinary drinking habits that explains the difference between their study and others.

The studies which have shown alcohol is protective have tended to be on very special populations. For example, the British doctors' study was all doctors; there was the nurses' study in the United States, the health professionals' study in the United States, and most famous of all, the study set up by the American Cancer Society, which was all volunteered. Now these people just don't have the same sort of drinking patterns as most punters, they're more likely to have this moderate, low intake, which doesn't seem to be detrimental and might even have some protective effects for coronary heart disease. But we just don't think that's the drinking pattern most people have.

Binge Drinking Is Harmful

Our study was in a representative population of people across the West of Scotland who had the drinking patterns which normal people have, and those drinking patterns in Britain (I don't know about Australia) are that you don't drink one or two glasses of wine every evening with your evening meal. What you do is, you don't drink during the week and then you go out and pour six or seven pints down your throat on Fridays and Saturdays, you binge drink on Fridays and Saturdays, obviously especially men at this time.

Now other populations which have been able to look at binge drinking show the same as us. So for example, there's a study in Finland, which showed that men who reported frequent hangovers had a higher rate of cardiovascular disease, it showed that the men who drank many pints of beer at a single sitting had a higher rate of cardiovascular disease, and of most importance for public health terms, is what's happening with cardiovascular disease mortality in the ex-Eastern Europe, where mortality rates have increased quite dramatically over the last six or eight years during a period when alcohol consumption, especially binge drinking, increased dramatically over that time. So in Russia, where people binge drink, certainly drinking is related to higher rates of cardiovascular disease, and we think the drinking patterns of the Scottish men were like the drinking patterns in Finland and in Russia: they were binge drinking, and that's detrimental especially for stroke. And also physiological evidence shows people who drink large amounts of alcohol on regular occasions, their clotting function is stimulated, so their blood tends to clot more and will tend to achieve strokes. Also it's well known that alcohol consumption increases blood pressure. Randomised trials of randomising people to drinking more or less demonstrates that alcohol increases blood pressure, which is a very strong risk factor for stroke.

Excessive Drinking Is Harmful

Drinking too much alcohol can raise the levels of some fats in the blood (triglycerides). It can also lead to high blood pressure, heart failure and a high calorie intake. (Consuming too many calories can lead to obesity and a higher risk of developing diabetes.) Excessive drinking and binge drinking can lead to stroke. Other serious problems include fetal alcohol syndrome, cardiomyopathy, cardiac arrhythmia and sudden cardiac death.

American Heart Association, *Circulation*, 2001.

High rates of alcohol consumption also make the heart muscle more unstable, electrically unstable, so you can get heart arrhythmias which would lead to sudden cardiac death. But there's lots of physiological mechanisms which would link binge drinking to mortality from cardiovascular disease.

The Scottish Study Accounted for All Factors

Diseases like coronary heart disease, have many different causes, and are influenced by our social class, whether we smoke, what we eat, and how stressed we are.

Unlike many others, this study accounted for or controlled for, these many complicating factors to tease out the effect of alcohol alone.

We really measured all the potential factors which could

confound the association. Non-drinkers in previous studies have been unhealthy people. I mean, it would include people who had given up drinking because they were sick; they'd already got heart disease and the doctor told them to stop drinking. We measured whether people had heart disease, we did electrocardiograms on them. But some of the apparent protective effect of moderate alcohol consumption we think was because of confounding by these other factors, by the fact that the moderate drinkers had a better risk profile for cardiovascular disease for other reasons.

How did non-drinkers stand up in the study?

Non-drinkers did well in our study, and one reason we think for that is that we think in this study, because it was working men, just men who could actually go to work, we didn't include a large number of people who were sick, and the reason they weren't drinking was because of health problems.

People's eyes start to glaze over when they're told that alcohol could be bad or good for them, according to different research outcomes. What should they be listening to?

I don't think the evidence overall would suggest that if you don't enjoy drinking you should drink for your health because of this notion that drinking protects against coronary heart disease. If you enjoy moderate drinking, moderate drinking is fine, but you should do it because you like it not because of its health effects. But pouring seven or eight pints down your throat on a Friday and Saturday night isn't good for you, so that's a very clear message and it can be not good for you in devastating ways: strokes in young males have been related to this pattern of binge drinking, and a stroke in a young bloke is a sort of devastating event.

Could moderate drinking feasibly protect us against coronary heart disease, or is that still unestablished?

I think there's some feasible reasons why moderate drinking may have a protective effect against coronary heart disease. I think that it's not definitely established and also the messages that promote drinking as being healthy aren't going to just increase moderate drinking, they're going to also increase heavy drinking at the heavy end of the spectrum.

So people will justify their drinking habits?

Yes, absolutely, just like I do.

"To fail to inform . . . patients about the benefits of moderate drinking is both counterproductive and dishonest."

Doctors Should Encourage Their Patients to Use Alcohol

Stanton Peele

In the following viewpoint Stanton Peele argues that moderate drinking has been proven to be beneficial to health and, therefore, doctors should encourage their patients to use alcohol. He dismisses the argument that providing information about the benefits of drinking will cause people to abuse alcohol. Peele maintains that doctors have an obligation to inform their patients of all treatment options—patients are capable of making the best choices for their own treatment. Stanton Peele, a psychologist and researcher specializing in drug and alcohol addiction, is the author of *The Diseasing of America: How We Allowed Recovery Zealots and the Treatment Industry to Convince Us We Are Out of Control.*

As you read, consider the following questions:
1. According to Peele, what should doctors do if patients are incapable of regulating their own diets, drinking, and exercise?
2. What drinking levels do U.S. guidelines suggest lower death rates?
3. Why does Peele argue that patients should drink only at moderate levels?

Stanton Peele, "Should Physicians Recommend Alcohol to Their Patients?" *Priorities for Health*, vol. 8, 1997, pp. 24–28. Copyright © 1997 by the American Council on Science and Health (ACSH), www.acsh.org. Reproduced by permission.

Whenever I have visited a physician over the last decade, the following scenario has been replayed: we discuss my cholesterol levels (total, LDL, and HDL). We review diet guidelines and other medical recommendations. Then I say, "Don't forget to remind me to drink a glass or two of wine daily." Invariably, the physician demurs: "That hasn't been proven to protect you against atherosclerosis."

My doctors, all of whom I have respected and liked, are wrong. Evidence has established beyond question that alcohol reduces coronary artery disease, America's major killer. This result has been found in the Harvard Physician and Nurse studies and in studies by Kaiser Permanente and the American Cancer Society (ACS). Indeed, the evidence that alcohol reduces coronary artery disease and mortality is better than the evidence for the statin drugs, the most potent cholesterol-reducing medications.

Drinking to excess does increase mortality from several sources, such as cancer, cirrhosis, and accidents. But a series of studies in the 1990s—including those conducted in conjunction with Kaiser, ACS, and Harvard—in the U.S., Britain, and Denmark, have found that moderate drinking reduces *overall* mortality.

Nonetheless, many object to the idea that doctors should inform their patients that moderate drinking may prolong life. They fear that such advice will justify the excessive drinking some patients already engage in, or they worry that encouragement from doctors will push people who cannot handle alcohol to drink.

The view that people are so stupid or malleable that they will become alcohol abusers because doctors tell them that moderate drinking is good for them is demeaning and self-defeating. If people can't regulate their own diets, drinking, and exercise, then doctors should avoid giving patients *any* information about their health behavior, no matter how potentially helpful.

Not only can people handle such information on lifestyle, it offers the primary and best way to attack heart disease. Of course, doctors may also prescribe medications. These medications rarely solve underlying problems, however; and they often cause adverse side effects that counterbalance their positive effects. Because they are not a cure, courses of medication, once begun, are rarely discontinued.

Most Americans Drink Less than Is Healthful

People are the best regulators of their own behaviors. Even those who drink excessively often benefit when doctors provide straightforward, accurate information. Clinical trials conducted by the World Health Organization around the world showed that so-called brief interventions, in which medical personnel advised heavy drinkers to reduce their drinking, are the *most* successful therapy for problem drinking.

But far more Americans drink *less*, not more, than would be most healthful for them. To fail to inform these patients about the benefits of moderate drinking is both counterproductive and dishonest. Physicians may ask, "How much alcohol do you drink," "Is there any reason that you don't drink (or drink so little)," and (to those without religious objections, previous drinking problems, etc.), "Do you know that one or two glasses of wine or beer a day can be good for your health, if you can safely consume them?"

Here are the data about alcohol and mortality:

1. In 1995 Charles Fuchs and his colleagues at Harvard found that women who drank up to two drinks a day lived longer than abstainers. Subjects were 85,700 nurses.

2. In 1995, Morten Gronbæk and colleagues found that wine drinkers survived longer than abstainers, with those drinking three to five glasses daily having the lowest death rate. Subjects were 20,000 Danes.

3. In 1994, Richard Doll and his colleagues found that men who drank up to two drinks daily lived significantly longer than abstainers. Subjects were 12,300 British doctors.

4. In 1992, Il Suh and colleagues found a 40 percent reduction in coronary mortality among men drinking three and more drinks daily. The 11,700 male subjects were in the upper 10 to 15 percent of risk for coronary heart disease. Alcohol's enhancement of high density lipoproteins was identified as the protective factor.

5. In 1990, Paolo Boffetta and Lawrence Garfinkel found that men who drank occasionally—up to two drinks daily—outlived abstainers. Subjects were over a quarter of a million

volunteers enrolled by the American Cancer Society.

6. In 1990, Arthur Klatsky and his colleagues found that those who drank one or two drinks daily had the lowest overall mortality rate. Subjects were 85,000 Kaiser Permanente patients of both genders and all races.

Guidelines Are Open to Dispute

These data—from large prospective studies of people of both sexes, different occupations, several nations, and varying risk profiles—all point to alcohol's life-sustaining effects. This phenomenon is now so well accepted that the U.S. *Dietary Guidelines* released in January 1996 recognize that moderate drinking can be beneficial.

Handelsman. © 2003 by Tribune Media Services. Reprinted with permission.

The levels of drinking at which alcohol lowers death rates are still open to dispute. The new U.S. guidelines indicate that men should not drink more than two drinks per day and women should not exceed one per day. But the British government has set its limits for "sensible drinking" at three to four drinks for men and two to three drinks for women [these drinks are somewhat smaller, however]. That abstemiousness increases the risk of death, however, can no longer be doubted.

Moreover, alcohol operates at least as effectively as pharmaceuticals to reduce the risk of death for those at high risk for coronary disease.

At one point, researchers questioned whether people who had quit drinking due to previous health problems inflated the mortality rate among abstainers. But this position can no longer be maintained. The studies described above separate drinkers who have quit drinking and who had pre-existing health problems from other nondrinkers. The benefits of drinking persisted with these individuals omitted.

At some point, ranging from three to six drinks daily, the negative effects of drinking for cancer, cirrhosis, and accidents catch up to and surpass alcohol's beneficial cardiac impact. Moreover, women under 50—who have relatively low rates of heart disease and relatively high rates of breast cancer mortality—may not benefit from drinking. That is, unless they have one or more cardiac risk factors.

Even younger women with such risk factors benefit from light to moderate drinking. And, we must remember, *most* American women and men have such risk factors. (Fuchs et al. found about three-quarters of the nurses in the Harvard study had at least one.) Remember, over all ages, American women are ten times as likely to die of heart disease (40%) as of breast cancer (4%).

Why, then, do Americans—physicians, public health workers, educators, and political leaders—refuse to recognize alcohol's benefits? We might also ask why the United States banned the manufacture, sale, and transportation of alcoholic beverages from 1920 to 1933. It is probably too obvious to mention that alcohol has never been banned—or prohibition even seriously discussed—in France, Italy, Spain and a number of other European nations.

Americans See Alcohol in a Negative Light

What is it about America and some other nations that prevents them from considering that alcohol may be good for people? These so called "temperance" nations, which see alcohol in a highly negative light. This is true even though nations with higher alcohol consumption have lower death rates from coronary heart disease (see Table 1). Oddly, temperance nations—despite concentrating on alcohol problem prevention and treatment—actually have *more* drinking problems than those in which alcohol is socially accepted and integrated.

Table 1. Temperance, Alcohol Consumption, and Cardiac Mortality

Alcohol Consumption (1990)	Temperance Nations[a]	Non-Temperance Nations[b]
total consumption[c]	6.6	10.8
percent wine	17.7	43.7
percent beer	53.1	40.4
percent spirits	29.2	15.9
AA groups/million population	170	25
coronary mortality[d] (males 50–64)	421	272

[a]Norway, Sweden, U.S., U.K., Ireland, Australia, New Zealand, Canada, Finland, Iceland

[b]Italy, France, Spain, Portugal, Switzerland, Germany, Denmark, Austria, Belgium, Luxembourg, Netherlands

[c]Liters consumed per capita per year

[d]Deaths per 100,000 population

Source: Stanton Peele, *Culture, Alcohol, and Health: The Consequences of Alcohol Consumption Among Western Nations*, December 1, 1995.

This occurs even though temperance nations drink less alcohol. But they drink a higher percentage of their alcohol in the form of spirits. This drinking is more likely to take place in concentrated bursts among men at sporting events or in drinking establishments. This style of drinking contrasts with that in wine-drinking nations, which encourage socialized drinking among family members of both genders and all ages at meals and other social gatherings. These cultures do not teach people that alcohol is an addictive drug. Rather, moderate drinking is modeled for children and taught to them in the home. Furthermore, these cultures accept that drinking may be good for you. We should too.

"It is not advisable . . . to recommend that those who have chosen to abstain from alcohol start drinking."

Doctors Should Not Encourage Their Patients to Use Alcohol

Charlotte LoBuono

In the following viewpoint Charlotte LoBuono argues that there is no conclusive data indicating that nondrinkers will derive health benefits from beginning to drink. However, she maintains that there is substantial data indicating that alcohol can be detrimental to health, and, therefore, doctors should not encourage their patients to drink. Instead, she contends, doctors should remind their patients that they can reduce cardiovascular risk in other medically proven ways. Charlotte LoBuono, a medical and health writer, was senior associate editor of *Patient Care* when she wrote this viewpoint. She is now senior associate editor of *Drug Topics*.

As you read, consider the following questions:
1. What does LoBuono argue is the effect of drinking alcohol with meals?
2. According to the author, how do the psychological symptoms of excessive drinking differ for men and women?
3. What percentage of patients seen by a primary care physician are estimated to use or be dependent on alcohol?

Charlotte LoBuono, "Dealing with the Alcohol Controversy," *Patient Care*, vol. 34, March 15, 2000, p. 211. Copyright © 2000 by *Patient Care*. Reproduced by permission.

Although the detrimental effects of excessive alcohol use are well-known, moderate drinking is now correlated with beneficial health effects in certain patient populations. Think twice, however, before telling patients that light alcohol use may be helpful.

Moderate amounts of alcohol have salutary effects, particularly on the cardiovascular system. The potential benefits of alcohol use include increased HDL cholesterol levels and prolonged clotting time, as well as reduced risk for coronary artery disease, adult-onset diabetes, and ischemic stroke. It is important to exercise caution, however, when discussing the benefits of light drinking with patients. Those who choose to abstain from alcohol, have a history of drinking problems, currently struggle with dependence, or who otherwise should not drink must not be encouraged to start (or continue) because they believe drinking will improve their health. Such patients should be identified before you offer information on the potential health benefits of moderate drinking.

Patients who may gain the most from moderate alcohol consumption are difficult to pinpoint. Those who are predisposed to cardiovascular disease, stroke, and diabetes may benefit from moderate alcohol consumption over the course of a lifetime. Persons who are at risk of these conditions and have demonstrated that they can drink within the limits of moderation should be able to continue to do so. . . .

Health Hazards of Drinking

Moderate drinkers are at some risk of alcohol-related disease and injury, but at less risk—obviously—than those who drink heavily. Even at relatively low levels, alcohol use has well-documented associations with hepatic diseases such as cancer and cirrhosis, as well as breast cancer, hemorrhagic stroke, hypertension, and depression.

The risk of cirrhosis can increase significantly with as few as 2 to 3 drinks per day. BP [blood pressure] may increase in someone who has 1 or 2 drinks daily Use of ethanol is also linked to cancers of the oral cavity, pharynx, larynx, and esophagus at even less than 1 drink per day. As few as 2 drinks a day increase the risk of hip fractures in women, and

2 to 3 drinks per day increase the risk of fatal injuries in both young women and men.

Immoderate ethanol consumption affects the metabolism of most nutrients. Heavy alcohol ingestion causes hypoglycemia and is associated with glucose intolerance as well. This effect is believed to be the result of inhibited insulin secretion. Ethanol misuse also induces protein loss, as well as an inhibition of intestinal protein absorption and an increase in urinary nitrogen excretion. Free fatty acid levels are decreased, and lipolysis is inhibited by chronic ethanol abuse. Heavy drinking may also increase serum triglyceride levels. Increased risk of physical injury, especially in automobile accidents, is an established possible consequence of alcohol misuse.

What is moderate or safe alcohol consumption? A standard drink in the United States is 12 oz of beer, 5 oz of wine, or 1.5 oz of spirits. Each of these portions contains a similar amount of alcohol. The amount deemed safe is no more than 1 standard-sized drink per day for women and 2 standard-sized drinks per day for men. Amounts in excess of these are associated with an increased risk of morbidity and mortality. Patients should be aware of other guidelines as well. Women, for example, should not take more than 3 drinks per occasion, and men should not take more than 4 drinks. Those who drink more than this are at risk for future alcohol-related consequences.

People who drink with meals are more likely to drink responsibly and less likely to become intoxicated, and the ingestion of food with alcohol does not seem to diminish the benefits of alcohol. When alcohol is consumed with food, however, less ethanol is absorbed and at a slower rate, reducing any harmful hepatic effects. A beneficial interaction between the nutrients in food and alcohol is possible, but further investigation is needed. . . .

Excessive drinking can also increase the risk of stroke. A study in the journal *Circulation* found a strong dose-response relationship between alcohol consumption and risk of 3 subtypes of stroke. . . .

Psychosocial complications such as belligerence, problems in the workplace, and difficulties with interpersonal relationships can be attributed to heavy alcohol consumption. Symptoms that men who abuse alcohol display may differ from those seen in women. For example, whereas men with alcohol problems may behave more aggressively and experience difficulties at work, women may have more difficulty in social relationships.

Alcohol and Women's Health

Some physicians may overlook the possibility of alcohol abuse among their female patients. As many as 5% of American women are estimated to suffer from alcohol abuse and dependence. Ethanol abuse is characterized by a poor performance at school or work, including alcohol-related absences; neglected personal responsibilities; use of alcohol in dangerous circumstances, for example, while driving; and continued drinking despite increasing personal problems related to excessive use of alcohol. Dependence encompasses all the above criteria as well as tolerance, withdrawal, and compulsive behavior related to alcohol abuse.

Approximately 25% of women have had a problem related to alcohol abuse at some point in their lives. In addition, 9% of women who visit a primary care physician have had an alcohol-related problem in the past year, although women are half as likely as men to have received treatment for alcohol problems. On the basis of these statistics, alcohol dependence is clearly a significant health issue for women. The problem may not be readily apparent, however, because women may have more difficulty than men admitting to the abuse of alcohol. . . .

A public health study confirmed previous research that, at least among white women, biological and psychosocial factors place women at greater risk for alcohol-related health problems and intoxication than men consuming similar amounts of alcohol. Women achieve a higher blood alcohol concentration than men when given the same absolute quantity of alcohol per pound of body weight because women's bodies have a higher fat and lower water content than men's bodies. Metabolism of alcohol by the stomach is less efficient in women than in men. Alcoholic men are less likely than their female counterparts to suffer from suicide, anemia, circulatory disease, and hepatic cirrhosis linked to alcohol abuse.

Women may be more vulnerable to alcohol-associated psychological problems than men because of the greater social stigma associated with female drunkenness. Women who are drunk may be perceived as sexually promiscuous or neglectful of their families and homes. Male intoxication may be associated with less of a stigma because it is consistent with so-called masculine traits, including risk taking, physical stamina, and personal prowess.

The American Heart Association Does Not Recommend Alcohol

Over 60 clinical studies have suggested that light to moderate alcohol consumption (the equivalent of one 1½ oz. of alcohol per day) can increase HDL cholesterol levels (the "good" cholesterol) by approximately 12%, and can reduce the incidence of myocardial infarction.

However, excessive alcohol consumption reliably causes a number of severe medical problems including auto accidents, cardiomyopathy and heart failure, liver failure, stroke, and cancer, not to mention the destructive social pathologies associated with alcoholism itself. . . .

In addition, many have argued that it may not be the alcohol itself that provides the benefit, but the "company" alcohol keeps. It has been postulated, for instance, that people who enjoy a glass of fine red wine with dinner may just have a relatively healthy lifestyle, or may belong to a relatively favorable socioeconomic class. Some studies have even suggested that substances in beer and wine other than the alcohol (such as flavenoids) might actually be the beneficial agent

For all these reasons, a special advisory panel of the American Heart Association issued a formal statement, published in January, 2001 in *Circulation*, urging doctors *not* to recommend alcohol to their patients as a means of reducing the risk of heart disease.

Richard N. Fogoros, "Uh, Oh. A Little Alcohol Really *Is* Good for the Heart," February 22, 2001. www.heartdisease.about.com.

According to the public health study mentioned above, Caucasian women were at greatest risk for experiencing alcohol-related problems as rates of heavier drinking increased. The study also found a greater sex disparity in the effects of heavier drinking among whites than blacks. One finding of this investigation, that black women are less vulnerable to problems related to drinking then are black men, has rarely been reported.

The Alcohol-Estrogen–Breast Cancer Link

Alcohol consumption, even in moderate amounts, may increase the risk of breast cancer in postmenopausal women taking estrogen replacement therapy (ERT) by increasing levels of circulating estradiol by as much as 300%. Evidence suggests that the use of both ERT and alcohol increases the risk of breast cancer more than the use of either one alone. Unfortunately many studies that evaluate the effect of alcohol consumption on breast cancer risk have not considered postmenopausal ERT use, and other studies to determine the influence of ERT on relative breast cancer risk have neglected to account for alcohol use. There does appear to be a dose-response effect, however, with relative risk increasing at a rate of approximately 10% per drink per day. Many studies have reported that consuming 1 or 2 drinks per day increases the risk of breast cancer. Alcohol has a similar effect on circulating estrogen levels in both pre-menopausal and postmenopausal women. . . .

[For women] moderate drinking decreases the risk of death from (CHD) [coronary heart disease] while heavier drinking increases the risk of mortality from other causes such as cirrhosis and breast cancer. Although moderate alcohol consumption is associated with reduced all-cause mortality in women, those at greatest risk for (CHD) benefit the most. This group includes elderly women and those with coronary risk factors. Younger women and women without coronary risk factors do not gain significant additional benefit from moderate drinking. In fact, drinking substantially increases their risk of mortality, as well as their risk of infertility, cirrhosis, and breast cancer, among other consequences. . . .

Although as many as 36% of patients seen by primary care physicians are estimated either to abuse alcohol or to be dependent on it, these disorders often go unrecognized. Questions concerning quantity and frequency of alcohol consumption can yield valuable insight when you suspect that a patient's injury or illness may be alcohol-related, as well as provide an early warning signal of abuse or addiction. Responses to inquiries about alcohol use can alert you to a patient at risk for a drinking problem, so that the mistake of recommending continued alcohol use by someone who should abstain can be averted. . . .

Do Not Recommend Alcohol

No data exist to prove that a population of nondrinkers will derive health benefits if they begin to drink moderately. It is not advisable therefore, to recommend that those who have chosen to abstain from alcohol start drinking. Those who do drink moderately should not increase their alcohol consumption. Patients with a personal or family history of alcohol-related problems as well as those with current problems should avoid alcoholic beverages. Remind patients that they can also reduce cardiovascular risk in other ways, such as by eating a healthy diet, exercising, and taking lipid-lowering drugs. Women who have a strong family history of or who are otherwise predisposed to breast cancer should limit alcohol, as should pregnant women, those trying to conceive, and people who drive or operate heavy machinery.

When discussing alcohol use with patients, use a cautious approach that is honest and succinct, emphasizing the importance of moderation and the potential dangers of alcohol abuse. Make sure patients understand the difficulty of drawing the line between safe and risky use—and how this might differ in men and women.

"By any public health standard, America has an epidemic of underage drinking."

Drinking Is a Serious Health Problem for Teens

Joseph A. Califano Jr.

Joseph A. Califano Jr. argues in the following viewpoint that underage drinking is implicated in teen overdose deaths, suicides, and accidents. Moreover, he maintains that teenagers who drink are more likely to engage in unprotected sex, leading to an increased risk of unwanted pregnancies and sexually transmitted diseases including AIDS. Since 1975 the age at which teens begin drinking has been steadily dropping, thus, underage drinking has become a significant public health issue. Joseph A. Califano Jr. is the chairman and president of the National Center on Addiction and Substance Abuse at Columbia University, a research-oriented organization that studies substance abuse and addiction.

As you read, consider the following questions:
1. According to the author, what percentage of high school students admit to binge drinking at least once a month?
2. In Califano's opinion, what are the three top causes of teen deaths?
3. What does Califano argue would happen to the alcohol industry without underage drinkers?

Joseph A. Califano Jr., "Teen Tipplers: America's Underage Drinking Epidemic," *Report by the National Center on Addiction and Substance Abuse at Columbia University*, February 26, 2002. Copyright © 2002 by the National Center on Addiction and Substance Abuse at Columbia University. Reproduced by permission.

Alcohol is far and away the top drug of abuse by America's teens. Children under the age of 21 drink 25 percent of the alcohol consumed in the U.S. More than five million high school students (31.5 percent) admit to binge drinking at least once a month. The age at which children begin drinking is dropping: since 1975, the proportion of children who begin drinking in the eighth grade or earlier has jumped by almost a third, from 27 to 36 percent. And the gender gap that for generations separated alcohol consumption by girls and boys has evaporated: male and female ninth graders are just as likely to drink (40.2 percent and 41 percent) and binge drink (21.7 percent and 20.2 percent).

By any public health standard, America has an epidemic of underage drinking that germinates in elementary and middle schools with children nine to 13 years old and erupts on college campuses where 44 percent of students binge drink and alcohol is the number one substance of abuse—implicated in date rape, sexual harassment, racial disturbances, drop outs, overdose deaths from alcohol poisoning and suicides. Teenagers who drink are seven times likelier to engage in sex and twice as likely to have sex with four or more partners than those who do not. Such behavior can lead to unprotected sex with the increased risk of AIDS, other sexually transmitted diseases and pregnancy. Preliminary studies have shown that alcohol damages young minds, limiting mental and social development. High schoolers who drink are five times likelier to drop out of school.

Alcohol Equals Fatal Attraction

No other substance threatens as many of the nation's children. Eighty percent of high school students have tried alcohol, while 70 percent have smoked cigarettes and 47 percent have used marijuana. Twenty-nine percent of high school seniors have used some other illegal drug such as Ecstasy.

Drinking is teen America's fatal attraction. Beer and other alcohol are implicated in the three top causes of teen deaths: accidents (including traffic fatalities and drowning), homicide and suicide. The financial costs of underage drinking approach $53 billion in accidents, drowning, burns, violent crime, suicide attempts, fetal alcohol syndrome, alcohol poisoning and emergency medical care. Teens who experiment with alcohol are virtually certain to continue using it. Among high school seniors who have ever tried alcohol—even once—91.3 percent are still drinking in twelfth grade. Most troubling, of high school students who have ever been drunk, 83.3 percent—more than two million teens—are still getting drunk in twelfth grade.

This report makes clear: the time and place to deal with binge drinking in college is in elementary and high school.

Teen drinking is the number one source of adult alcoholism. Children who begin drinking before age 21 are more than twice as likely to develop alcohol-related problems. Those who begin drinking before age 15 are four times likelier to become alcoholics than those who do not drink before age 21.

Underage drinkers are at greater risk of nicotine and illegal drug addiction. Teens who are heavy drinkers (consume at least five drinks on at least five occasions over 30 days) are more than 12 times likelier to use illegal drugs than those who do not drink.

How did we get here?

Adults Must Accept the Responsibility

We have to point the finger at ourselves.

Parents tend to see drinking and occasional bingeing as a rite of passage, rather than a deadly round of Russian roulette. Home—a child's or a child's friend's—is a major source of alcohol for children, especially for younger children. A third of sixth and ninth graders obtain alcohol from their own homes. Children cite other people's houses as the most common setting for drinking. In our schools, middle and high school teachers have been reluctant to inform parents or intervene when they suspect a child or teen of drinking. College administrators and alumni have played Pontius Pilate, washing their hands and looking away, as students made beer, alcohol and binge drinking a central part of their college experience. The pervasive influence of the entertainment media has glamorized and sexualized alcohol and rarely shown the ill effects of abuse. A review of 81 G-rated animated films found that in 34 percent of them alcohol use was associated with wealth or luxury and 19 percent associated alcohol with sexual activity.

Teen Drinking Is Increasing

More and more teens are drinking, the age at initial use is decreasing, and drinking rates among female teens are approaching those among males. Teen drinking rates should be of great concern, not only because of the dramatic costs of alcohol abuse to society (recently estimated at $148 billion), but also because alcohol remains the drug of choice for American teens, and continues to be associated with high rates or DUI convictions and fatal auto accidents. These are alarming trends, at a time when teen involvement in other types of substance abuse is decreasing.

Helen L. Johnson and Patrick B. Johnson, *Professional Counselor*, December 1999.

Television runs ads glorifying beer on sports programs watched by millions of children and teens. General Electric had decided that one of "the good things it will bring to life" will be hard liquor commercials on its NBC network. In its craven collaboration with the distilled spirits industry, GE has made NBC the only network to hawk hard liquor on shows watched by millions of children and teens. With a big push from alcohol lobbyists, the Congress has denied the White House Office of National Drug Control Policy authority to include alcohol—the number one drug of abuse by children and teens—in its media campaign and other activities to prevent drug abuse.

Underage Drinking Must Be Curbed

The interest of the alcohol industry—especially those who sell beer—in underage drinking is understandable, if appalling. Underage drinkers are a critical segment of the alcohol beverage market. Individuals who do not drink before age 21 are virtually certain never to do so: 82.8 percent of adults who drink had their first drink of alcohol before age 21. Underage drinkers consume 25 percent of the alcohol— most often beer—sold in this country. In 1998, they accounted for up to $27 billion of the $108 billion spent on alcohol, including as much as $15 billion on beer. Without underage drinkers, the alcohol industry, and the beer industry in particular, would suffer severe economic declines and dramatic loss of profits.

Drawn from CASA's [Center on Addiction and Substance Abuse] innovative National Underage Drinking Survey of adults, this report calls for a National Mobilization to curb underage drinking. It sets out actions for parents, law enforcement, legislators, the entertainment industry and for a measure of self-control by the beer, wine and liquor industries. It will take all of that to save millions of teens from destroying their lives through alcohol abuse. Our children are our future and, for adults, the future is now in mounting a national effort to curb teen drinking. This survey provides a road map of citizens' attitudes to guide federal, state and local officials interested in promoting public policies to reduce teen use of alcohol and binge drinking.

The prevention message is more difficult to convey with regard to alcohol. For smoking and illegal drug use, the message is, "No!" for children and adults. For alcohol, the message is "No!" for children under 21 (except for certain family and cultural occasions), but for most adults (those who are not alcoholics or alcohol abusers) the message is moderation, not prohibition.

*"College drinking rates have been falling
for two decades. . . . Drinking by high
school students and binge drinking have
also fallen."*

The Health Problems
Associated with Teen Drinking
Have Been Exaggerated

Doug Bandow

The health crisis caused by underage drinking proclaimed by
the National Center for Addiction and Substance Abuse at
Columbia (CASA) does not exist, Doug Bandow argues in the
following viewpoint. He contends that CASA's study is comprised of inaccurate statistics and erroneous conclusions that
merely serve to advance the group's prohibitionist agenda.
Bandow maintains that prohibiting teens from drinking will
not reduce alcohol-related problems among youth; rather,
parents should teach their teens to drink responsibly. Doug
Bandow is a senior fellow at the Cato Institute, a conservative
think tank, and a regular contributor to publications such as
Fortune magazine.

As you read, consider the following questions:
1. According to Bandow, what is Califano's plan for curbing
   underage drinking?
2. Why does Bandow argue that CASA's work is obviously
   driven by a prohibitionist agenda?
3. In the author's opinion, what does the experience of
   foreign countries suggest about minors drinking at
   home?

Doug Bandow, "Alcohol Abuse Study Is Junk Science," *Conservative Chronicle*, vol.
17, March 20, 2002, p. 6. Copyright © 2002 by Copley News Service. Reproduced
by permission of the author.

Nothing spurs government to action more than a crisis, and nothing suggests a crisis more than a dose of junk science. So it is with "America's Underage Drinking Epidemic," as proclaimed by the National Center for Addiction and Substance Abuse at Columbia [CASA].

With great fanfare, CASA announced that underage drinkers consume a quarter of all alcohol in the U.S., "a problem of epidemic proportion." This leads to a host of problems costing $53 billion a year: "alcohol-related traffic accidents, violent crime, burns, drowning, suicide attempts, alcohol poisonings, fetal alcohol syndrome and treatment for alcohol abuse."

CASA's president, Joseph Califano, called for "national mobilization to curb underage drinking." To do so he would target the adult market: prohibit sales in public places, limit alcohol outlets, restrict home delivery, ban alcohol sponsorship of athletic leagues, prohibit advertising, increase alcohol taxes, require warning labels, force the industry to fund critical ads and expand the Office of National Drug Control Policy to alcohol.

Indeed, there is little that he would not try. Perhaps banning kids from establishments, such as restaurants, which sell alcohol. Perhaps targeting parents, legal guardians, and spouses who serve those under 21.

Califano's agenda would be suspect even if his facts were right. But they aren't.

Califano's Claims Are Not Plausible

The claim that minors account for a quarter of all alcohol consumption isn't plausible. By one estimate, 12- to 20-year-olds would have to be averaging two drinks a day.

CASA cites the government's National Household Survey on Drug Abuse. However, the survey over-samples 12- to 20-year olds, who make up 38 percent of those polled, but only 15 percent of the population. CASA ignored this fact.

The Substance Abuse and Mental Health Services Administration estimates that underage drinking actually accounts for 11.4 percent of total alcohol consumption. And much of that reflects responsible use by young adults, from 18 to 20. Not that the facts matter to Califano, who responded to criticism by claiming that the federal survey was flawed: "There's a tremendous underestimate in reporting."

CASA put out a statement contending that the real rate of underage drinking was probably "30 percent or more." If guesses qualify as research, CASA shouldn't bother looking at the federal data. Why not rely an tarot cards or chicken gizzards instead? Alas, CASA has long been noted for its scare-mongering. Eight years ago, the organization released a similar report, warning of binge drinking, and "death, violence, rape, and the spread of sexually transmitted diseases" in its wake. Here, too, drinking was seen as reaching "epidemic proportions."

Binge Drinking Declines

Binge drinking among University of Florida students, and especially among men, has declined during the last two years, according to a new campus study.

Overall, the rate of binge drinking—five or more drinks at one sitting—fell from 46 percent in 1999 to 40 percent in 2001, a decline of 6 percent among UF students, the study shows.

Cathy Keen, *University of Florida News*, August 30, 2001.

In an analysis of that study, *Forbes* media critic senior editor Kathy McNamara-Meis found that statistics were old, "not credible," or simply "pulled from thin air." When Califano responded, she discovered that "many of Califano's summaries are inaccurate and some grossly distort my reporting."

Misstated Statistics

Health and Human Services Secretary Donna Shalala said that CASA had misstated government statistics. State University of New York (Potsdam) professor David Hanson observed that "If I were teaching a research class, I would use this CASA report as an example of what not to do."

CASA's scare-mongering is particularly curious since college drinking rates have been falling for two decades. In fact, college drinking is at an all-time low, down 7 percent over the last decade. Drinking by high school students and binge drinking also have fallen.

The group's work is obviously driven by the prohibitionist agenda of Califano, [former president] Jimmy Carter's secretary of health, education, and welfare. The report fails to distinguish between use and abuse: "Individuals who do not drink before age 21 are virtually certain never to do so." Is that good? Alcohol use generates benefits as well as costs.

The report pours special scorn on parents who "tend to see drinking and occasional bingeing as a right of passage, rather than a deadly round of Russian roulette. Home—a child's or a child's friend's—is a major source of alcohol for children, especially for younger children." Less than a quarter of parents prohibit their children from using until age 21.

Yet the experience of foreign countries suggests that kids who learn to drink at home are less likely to be problem users.

Particularly dubious is forbidding 18- to 20-year-olds to drink.

Many of these legal adults, who can vote, conclude contracts, be drafted, and smoke, will be unprepared for potentially dangerous experimentation in college. There is a marked difference between a 12-year-old and a 20-year-old drinking, and the latter doing so with responsible adults or college fraternity buddies.

Like most things in life, alcohol can be abused. But abuse is best discouraged by teaching people to drink responsibly. Which, sadly CASA's inaccurate scare-mongering makes more difficult.

Periodical Bibliography

The following articles have been selected to supplement the diverse views presented in this chapter.

Alcoholism and Drug Abuse Weekly	"Study Finds No Health Benefits from Alcohol," July 19, 1999.
Christina M. Anderson	"Drinking More Often May Be Good for the Heart," *Harvard Crimson*, January 13, 2003.
Mary Jane Ashley et al.	"Beyond Ischemic Heart Disease: Are There Other Health Benefits from Drinking?" *Contemporary Drug Problems*, Winter 2000.
Felice J. Freyer	"Binge Drinking Among College Students Holds Steady," *Providence Journal*, March 24, 2002.
Gregg Glaser	"You're Better Off with Beer," *All About Beer*, July 2002.
Sandra Goatcher	"Health Benefits and Risks of Moderate Alcohol Consumption," Alberta Alcohol and Drug Abuse Commission, May 2002. www.corp.aadac.com.
Catherine Golub	"A Toast to Better Health? The Heart May Say Yes, but the Head Hesitates," *Environmental Nutrition*, February 2001.
Elisabeth Holmgren	"Moderation Guidelines Around the World: Messages on Risks and Benefits," *Wines and Vines*, March 2003.
Michael Judge	"Drinks All Around," *Opinion Journal*, March 30, 2002.
Peter Kupper	"Revisiting the French Paradox," *Wine Enthusiast Magazine*, February 2003.
National Institutes of Health	"Frequency of Light-to-Moderate Drinking Reduces Heart Disease in Men," January 8, 2003. www.nih.gov.
Pain and Central Nervous System Week	"Study Finds Moderate Alcohol Consumption Could Reduce Risk," February 11, 2002.
Eric Single	"Moderate Alcohol Consumption—The Public Health Issues," Ottawa Symposium on Moderate Alcohol Consumption, November 16, 2000. www.ccsa.ca.
Michael Steel	"A Hearty Booze Battle," *National Journal*, June 9, 2001.
Gary Stix	"Should Physicians Tell Some Nondrinkers to Start?" *Scientific American*, July 17, 2001.
USA Today	"How Often You Drink, Not What, Cuts Heart Problems," January 8, 2003.

CHAPTER 2

What Are the Causes of Alcohol Abuse?

Chapter Preface

Alcohol abuse is a complex disorder; there is no simple explanation as to why some people develop problems with alcohol and others do not. Most research indicates that there are many biological and psychosocial factors that mutually influence each other and cause an individual to abuse alcohol. One of the areas scientists have been examining as they explore the many causes of alcohol disorders is the influence of family history. Laypeople as well as experts have long noted that alcoholism runs in families, and a genetic basis for alcoholism has been well established in the scientific community. However, genes alone cannot tell the complete story.

For example, research shows that most children of alcoholics do not develop problems with alcohol. In fact, there is a substantial range in alcohol use—from abstinence to abuse—among children of alcoholics. "Risk for alcoholism is clearly influenced by both genetic and environmental factors," maintains Kari Buck, an assistant professor of behavioral neuroscience in the Oregon Health and Science University School of Medicine. She adds, "An individual's genes are responsible for about 50 percent of their risk for alcoholism. Environmental factors, including whether or not they actually drink alcohol, makes up the other 50 percent of their risk."

In 1997 the National Institute on Alcohol Abuse and Alcoholism's *Ninth Special Report to the U.S. Congress on Alcohol Abuse and Alcoholism* identified several important ways in which children of alcoholics are different from children who do not have a family history of alcoholism. Children of alcoholics suffer a higher incidence of mental and behavioral disorders, experience more adverse family environments that often include poverty and abuse, and often lack a sensitivity to alcohol's intoxicating effects or have an increased sensitivity to its anxiety-reducing effects. Psychiatrist Marc Schuckit of the University of California at San Diego has done extensive research on high-risk sons of alcoholics and found that they "experience a decreased intensity of response to alcohol, suggesting that some people drink too much because they are getting less feedback from alcohol."

Researchers emphasize, however, that what is unique about these risk-producing characteristics is the way in which they interact with each other. Further, the way these factors play out in a child's life help determine if he or she will develop an alcohol disorder. For example, children of alcoholics often have difficult temperaments (trouble with self-regulation and socialization) due to lack of stability in the home. In addition, they are frequently subjected to poor parenting, such as low levels of emotional support and a lack of discipline. Together, these two factors place them at increased risk for difficulty or failure in school and emotional distress. In turn, this makes it more likely that they will develop friendships within a deviant peer group in which members are much more likely to use and misuse alcohol.

As scientists identify risk factors for alcohol abuse and alcoholism, they hope to find potential moderators of these risks. Their ultimate goal is to develop interventions that target the risks of developing an alcohol use disorder caused by a family history of alcoholism. There is no simple answer to the question of what causes alcohol abuse and alcoholism. A family history of alcoholism is just one possibility. Authors in the following chapter explore other aspects of this complex and often baffling disorder as they debate the causes of alcohol abuse.

> "The risk that a person would develop
> alcohol abuse . . . was more than doubled
> for persons who began drinking before age
> 15 compared with those who began
> drinking at age 21."

Drinking at an Early Age Leads to Alcohol Abuse

National Institutes of Health

People who begin drinking before the age of fifteen are at a substantially greater risk of developing an alcohol disorder than those who do not imbibe until they are twenty-one or older, editors from the National Institutes of Health (NIH) argue in the following viewpoint. Moreover, the NIH contends that the overall risk for alcoholism decreases 14 percent with each year of age that drinking is postponed. The NIH, a division of the U.S. Department of Health and Human Services, is comprised of eighteen different research institutes including the National Institute on Alcohol Abuse and Alcoholism.

As you read, consider the following questions:
1. In the NIH's opinion, what is the difference between alcoholism and alcohol abuse?
2. According to HHS Secretary Donna E. Shalala, what message concerning underage drinking should parents, schools, and communities be giving to young people?
3. Editors argue that the risk for lifetime alcohol abuse decreases by what percentage with each increasing year of age of drinking onset?

National Institutes of Health, "Age of Drinking Onset Predicts Future Alcohol Abuse and Dependence," www.nih.gov, January 14, 1998. Copyright © 1998 by National Institutes of Health. Reproduced by permission.

The younger the age of drinking onset, the greater the chance that an individual at some point in life will develop a clinically defined alcohol disorder, according to a new report released [in January 14, 1998] by the National Institute on Alcohol Abuse and Alcoholism (NIAAA).

Young people who began drinking before age 15 were four times more likely to develop alcohol dependence (alcohol addiction, commonly known as alcoholism) than those who began drinking at age 21, researchers found. The risk that a person would develop alcohol abuse (a maladaptive drinking pattern that repeatedly causes life problems) was more than doubled for persons who began drinking before age 15 compared with those who began drinking at age 21.

The analysis by Bridget F. Grant, Ph.D., and Deborah A. Dawson, Ph.D., of NIAAA's Division of Biometry and Epidemiology, is published in the January [1998] issue of the *Journal of Substance Abuse* and based on the NIAAA-sponsored National Longitudinal Alcohol Epidemiologic Survey (NLAES), a national probability sample of nearly 43,000 interviews with field work conducted by the U.S. Census Bureau in 1992. NLAES is the survey from which NIAAA in 1995 reported the most recent national estimates of alcohol abuse and dependence.

"This study adds new evidence about the need to regard underage drinking as the serious problem it is," said HHS [Health and Human Services] Secretary Donna E. Shalala. . . .

"This first comprehensive analysis of the relationship between the age of drinking onset and the prevalence of lifetime alcohol abuse and dependence is one piece of a complex puzzle," said NIAAA director Enoch Gordis, M.D. "It remains to be seen whether it is the delay in alcohol use or, possibly, other associated factors that explain the inverse relationship between age at drinking onset and lifetime risk for alcohol abuse and alcoholism."

More than 40 percent of respondents who began drinking before age 15 were classified with alcohol dependence at some time in their lives, the researchers found. That compares to 24.5 percent for respondents who began drinking at age 17 and approximately 10 percent for respondents who began drinking at the ages of 21 and 22. The analysis revealed an in-

Early Onset Drinking Linked to Increased Injuries

Early onset of drinking increases frequent heavy drinking which in turn heightens risk of alcohol related injuries among persons under the legal drinking age of 21 and among adults over age 21 not only for persons with diagnosable alcohol dependence, but other drinkers as well. Further, those who begin drinking at an early age report more often placing themselves ever, and in the past year, in situations after drinking that increase risk of injury. That was found not only among alcohol dependents and others who more frequently drink heavily and to intoxication but other drinkers as well. Physicians and other health care providers should counsel their patients who start drinking at an early age not only about their increased risk for alcohol dependence, but also their increased risk of experiencing unintentional injury under the influence of alcohol.

Recent national surveys indicate that after a decade of decline, the percentage of high school seniors who drink, drink heavily and drive after drinking has increased [since 1999].

"Age of Onset and Unintentional Injury Involvement After Drinking," January 2001. www.nhtsa.dot.gov.

crease in risk for subsequent alcohol dependence among persons who began drinking at ages 23 and 24 that declined again for persons 25 and older. Overall, the risk for alcohol dependence decreased by 14 percent with each increasing year of age of drinking onset.

Similarly, the prevalence of alcohol abuse declined as the drinking age rose. Of those who began drinking at age 14, 13.8 percent subsequently were classified with alcohol abuse, compared with 2.5 percent of those who began drinking at age 25 and older. Overall, the risk for lifetime alcohol abuse decreased by 8 percent with each increasing year of age of drinking onset.

"The most significant contribution of this study is the focus it provides for future research on the interaction of personal and environmental factors in the development of alcohol abuse and alcoholism," said Gordis. "Fortunately, this report comes at a time when NIAAA has stringently tested and proved effective several preventive interventions that can be applied in schools and communities."

"It is almost certainly not adolescent or childhood drinking per se that leads to adulthood drinking problems."

Drinking at an Early Age Does Not Lead to Alcohol Abuse

Dwight B. Heath

Factors that predispose children and teens to underage drinking and other deviant behaviors are most likely responsible for adult drinking problems, not the age when they begin to imbibe, Dwight B. Heath argues in the following viewpoint. He contends that in cultures where it is acceptable for young people to drink, teens and even young children consume alcohol without adverse consequences. In contrast, Americans preach "just say no" to their children, thereby making alcohol a "forbidden fruit" and encouraging youth to use it irresponsibly, he maintains. Dwight B. Heath is a professor of anthropology at Brown University and the author of *Drinking Occasions: Comparative Perspectives on Alcohol and Culture.*

As you read, consider the following questions:

1. Why does Heath maintain that the statistical relationship between the early age of drinking onset and later alcohol abuse is not proof of cause and effect?
2. According to Heath, why do American teens consider the use of alcohol a demonstration of maturity or a way to become more sociable, sexy, dynamic, or powerful?
3. In Heath's opinion, what do youngsters learn about alcohol in communities where early socialization to drinking is the norm?

Dwight B. Heath, "Should We 'Just Say No' to Childhood Drinking?" *Priorities for Health*, vol. 12, 2000, pp. 13–15. Copyright © 2000 by the American Council of Science and Health. Reproduced by permission of the American Council on Science and Health (ACSH), www.acsh.org.

E arly [in 2000] the American print media amply reported another in a long trail of negative announcements regarding alcoholic-beverage consumption. The press release that had triggered this wave of alcohol reportage, with its somber extrapolations, had grown out of a research project sponsored by the U.S. National Institute on Alcohol Abuse and Alcoholism (NIAAA). This study, published in the *Journal of Substance Abuse*, had concerned the correlation of (1) age of first beverage alcohol intake and (2) alcoholism. Its principal finding was, in simple terms, that subjects who had first imbibed at an early age were, to a statistically significant degree, likelier eventually to become alcoholics than were those who hadn't.

It is no secret that correlation often has little bearing on causation, yet many print journalists treated this finding as if it were dramatic proof that alcoholic beverage consumption is highly addictive and that it is dangerous for anyone under age 21. The same finding might be counterintuitive to anyone conversant with life in modern Europe or among Orthodox Jews. In Europe, frequently individuals are first invited to drink at an early age, but rates of alcohol dependence tend to be very low. Orthodox Jewish males are commonly given a taste of wine on the occasion of their circumcision—eight days after their birth. And many followers of that faith—youngsters as well as adults—drink wine ceremonially at least twice a week. But rates of drinking-related problems among Orthodox Jews are remarkably low.

NIAAA Findings Are Only Correct for America

Indeed, the NIAAA finding does not apply in most parts of the world outside the United States—where, alas, the finding is altogether reasonable. At least some of the efforts of the new temperance movement—i.e., the efforts of a loose, variegated coalition of activists trying to reduce beverage-alcohol consumption by humans categorically—evidently have been counterproductive.

Childhood drinking is deviant in the U.S.; in many states it is also illegal. One would reasonably expect that in such a setting underage drinkers would consist almost entirely of persons who freely behave in other deviant (e.g., risky or illegal) ways, in some cases deliberately. By the same token, one would reasonably expect that law-abiding, conformist youngsters who tend to avoid risks would also tend to defer drinking at least until adulthood. In other words, it is almost certainly not adolescent or childhood drinking per se that leads to adulthood drinking problems; it is far likelier that factors that predispose children and adolescents to deviant drinking and to other such behaviors are responsible.

European Parents Teach Moderation

In Americanized societies, parents often emphasize that drinking is a bad thing and that one should avoid it at all costs. However, the fact is that people are likely to start drinking during adolescence around friends. Parents are aware of this, however they cannot do much about it except trust the judgement of their children. Even then, many parents ignore this and pretend that the problem does not exist. In the European societies, it is often typical to introduce wines in small amounts during meals at a young age. By doing so, wine becomes a normal part of everyday life. The main difference between the two cultures is the role parents play in teaching children. Here, parents often do not teach their children what is right and what is not, apart from "alcohol is bad." Then, these same parents are shocked when they find out that their children drink. In European countries, parents introduce wine and are able to show their children what is the proper attitude when it comes to alcohol—moderation. The youth are then able to make wiser choices.

Jason Nery, Conflict Resolution Forum Website, February 6, 2000. www.garneteye.com.

Yet advocates of the new temperance movement have structured the relationship in the U.S. between childhood drinking and adulthood drinking problems so that the former phenomenon appears almost always to result in the latter!

In most parts of the world, beverage alcohol lacks the "forbidden fruit" appeal that invites its use by youngsters as a demonstration of maturity and/or as a means of becoming sociable, sexy, dynamic, or more powerful. Where children are not "protected from alcohol," their behavior suggests no need for such protection. These children take up drinking in relatively supportive surroundings (usually in their homes and among adult members of their families) as a wholesome and enjoyable part of everyday life—rather than as an illicit, surreptitious consequence of peer pressure.

Alcohol-Related Problems Are Not Caused by Early Drinking

As an anthropologist, I often deal with patterns of populations that are small, isolated, or tribal and whose characteristic beliefs and behaviors would not be feasible in industrial or post-industrial communities. But some of the best illustrations of my case concern the present-day middle classes of France, Italy, Spain, and other developed countries. Through official statistics from such countries, on such well-studied communities, I have repeatedly demonstrated that the incidence of so-called alcohol-related problems (physiological, psychological, social, economic, etc.) is inversely related both to "age of onset" (i.e., how early in one's life one first imbibes) and to average per capita consumption of beverage alcohol. This is just the opposite of what is claimed by the World Health Organization, the NIAAA, and other organizations primarily concerned with restricting alcoholic-beverage availability as a public health policy.

The same climate that almost guarantees that underage American drinkers will be otherwise deviant and will flout the law also virtually ensures that they will often drink furtively and excessively or rashly, and that they will do so among peers ignorant or unmindful of the specific long- and short-term risks of alcohol abuse—peers who may be reluctant to summon an adult in the event of an acute problem.

The "Just Say No" approach thus invites troubles.

In communities in which early socialization to drinking is the norm (i.e., in most communities), youngsters learn simultaneously how to drink moderately, how and why to avoid drunkenness, that drinking will not magically improve one's personality, and that excessive drinking illustrates weakness.

In short, the theory that early drinking leads to drinking problems is correct—but only in those few communities in which the normative and legal systems make the theory correct.

For anyone for whom such cross-cultural evidence is not

compelling, I recommend reading an article whose authors used a statistical methodology similar to that used by most of those who publish in support of the above-mentioned theory: "Age at First Drink and Risk for Alcoholism: A Noncausal Association," published last year [1999] in the prestigious journal *Alcoholism: Clinical and Experimental Research.*

"It [is] clear that alcoholism is a genetically complex disorder, influenced by multiple genes."

Alcoholism Has a Genetic Basis

National Institute on Alcohol Abuse and Alcoholism

Researchers from the National Institute on Alcohol Abuse and Alcoholism (NIAAA) argue that alcoholism is a genetically complex disorder, influenced by multiple genes interacting with each other and environmental factors to produce the disease. They maintain further that while alcoholism always has a genetic basis, individuals in different families will develop alcoholism under the influence of different predisposing genes. Genetic studies on alcoholism can lead the way to better treatments and prevention methods, the researchers contend. The NIAAA is part of the National Institutes of Health—a division of the U.S. Department of Health and Human Services—and conducts research focused on improving the treatment and prevention of alcoholism and alcohol-related problems.

As you read, consider the following questions:

1. According to NIAAA researchers, what do the newest studies reveal about the genetic influence of alcoholism in women?
2. In the researchers' opinion, about what fraction of the risk of becoming an alcoholic is genetically mediated?
3. What aspect of genetic studies do researchers argue will give them the most help in improving the treatment and prevention of alcoholism?

National Institute on Alcohol Abuse and Alcoholism, "Recent Progress in the Genetics of Alcoholism," *10th Special Report to the U.S. Congress on Alcohol and Health*, June 2000.

A t the time of publication of the *Ninth Special Report to the U.S. Congress on Alcohol and Health* (National Institute on Alcohol Abuse and Alcoholism 1997), twin, family, and adoption studies had very firmly established major roles for both genetics and environment in the etiology of alcoholism in men. Although the earlier studies had failed to detect a genetic component of alcoholism in women, the newest studies at that time were beginning to suggest that alcoholism is as strongly genetically influenced in women as it is in men. Since alcoholism does not follow the simple rules of Mendelian inheritance in multi-generational pedigrees, it was clear that alcoholism is a genetically complex disorder, influenced by multiple genes (their precise number unknown) that interact in an unknown fashion with each other and with similarly unknown environmental factors to produce the disease. It also seemed highly likely that alcoholism is genetically heterogeneous, meaning that individuals in different families develop alcoholism under the influence of different predisposing genes. . . .

Just two of the genes influencing predisposition to alcoholism were known. A defective allele (variant) of the gene *ALDH2*, common in Asian populations, had long been known to substantially (although not completely) protect carriers from developing alcoholism by making them uncomfortable or ill after drinking alcohol. The *ALDH2* gene encodes aldehyde dehydrogenase, one of the two key liver enzymes involved in the metabolism of alcohol to its final end product, acetate. The illness resulting from the defective allele tended to prevent carriers from drinking enough alcohol to become addicted to it. Newer studies were beginning to suggest that alleles of *ADH2* and *ADH3*, genes encoding two forms of liver alcohol dehydrogenase (the enzyme that carries out the first step in alcohol metabolism in the liver), also protected carriers from developing alcoholism, albeit to a lesser extent than did the defective allele of *ALDH2*. The protective alleles of *ADH2* and *ADH3*, also common in Asian populations, encode forms of alcohol dehydrogenase that metabolize alcohol to acetaldehyde more rapidly than other forms of these enzymes do. This rapid metabolism leads to a greater buildup of this toxic product in the bloodstream after consumption of alcohol, thereby producing feelings of discomfort and illness and tending to discourage carriers of these alleles from consuming large amounts of alcohol.

Finally, there was a large controversy about the role in the etiology of alcoholism of a particular allele of *DRD2*, a gene encoding a particular form of brain receptor for dopamine. Dopamine is a neurotransmitter that plays a central role in brain pathways and that mediates the rewarding properties of alcohol and other drugs of abuse. While a large number of papers had concluded that this allele was associated with alcoholism, an even larger number of papers had reached the contrary conclusion. Questions were raised about the methodological validity of a number of the studies and their corresponding findings, the reasons for the inconsistent findings, and—even when the validity of some of the findings was assumed—their precise biological significance.

Twin/Family Studies Provide Important Data

The classic twin study design compares the resemblances for a trait of interest between monozygotic (MZ, identical) twins and dizygotic (DZ, fraternal) twins, in order to determine the extent of genetic influence, or heritability, of the trait. Heritability can be calculated because MZ twins are genetically identical, whereas DZ twins share only half their genes. The method relies on the "equal-environment assumption," that is, that the similarity between the environments of both individuals in a pair of MZ twins is the same as the similarity between the environments of members of pairs of DZ twins. While earlier twin studies have been severely criticized for not testing this assumption sufficiently, researchers have taken care more recently to collect data on the twins' environments, thereby allowing correction of results for any deviation from this assumption. While twin studies do not identify specific genes influencing a trait, they do provide important information on the trait's genetic architecture (more general properties of its inheritance pattern, such as whether genes act independently of one another, or in concert, to influence a trait), which aspects of the trait are most heritable, whether the same genes are influencing the trait in both genders, and whether multiple traits share any common genetic influences. When data on twins are augmented by data on their family members, the study is termed a twin/family study and can provide more precise information about whether parents transmit a behavioral trait to their offspring genetically or via some aspect of the familial environment (cultural transmission). When detailed data about the environment are collected, twin and twin/family studies can provide information about how environmental factors interact with genetic predisposition to produce a disease.

The Genetic Link to Alcoholism Is Complex

The blueprint for the human body is encoded in its genes. Genes govern the expression of specific genetic traits and account for trait differences that help distinguish one individual from another. Each gene directs the synthesis of a different protein. Abnormal gene variants may give rise to defective proteins that can contribute to disease. Vulnerability to complex diseases like alcoholism requires changes in multiple genes. Because genetics studies indicate that between 40 and 60 percent of alcoholism vulnerability has a genetic basis, finding the genes that are involved in alcoholism vulnerability is a high priority for alcohol research. Genetics studies, such as the *Collaborative Study on the Genetics of Alcoholism*, have already identified several sites in the brain where the genes for alcoholism may be located. The map of the human genome will no doubt help lead investigators to the discovery of the genes that play a role in increasing an individual's vulnerability to alcoholism.

National Institute on Alcohol Abuse and Alcoholism, *Alcohol Alert*, July 2000.

While earlier twin studies have firmly established substantial heritability of alcoholism in men (on the order of 50 percent), they have generally failed to detect heritability in women. This failure may be due, in part, to the lower rate of alcoholism among women than men, thereby necessitating larger sample sizes to achieve statistically significant results. Since the first studies to report a substantial heritability of alcoholism in women, others have reported analysis of a sample of volunteer adult Australian twins consisting of 1,328 MZ pairs and 1,357 DZ pairs (distributed among all possible combinations of genders). Of these subjects, about 25 percent of the men and about 6 percent of the women met

DSM-IIIR criteria for alcohol dependence. (DSM-IIIR refers to the *Diagnostic and Statistical Manual of Mental Disorders, Third Edition, Revised,* a standard classification system for mental disorders.) Analysis of the concordances for alcoholism among the various classes of twins suggested that about two-thirds of the risk of becoming alcoholic was genetically mediated in both men and women, with the remainder of the risk determined by environmental factors not shared by the two members of a given twin pair. The data provided no evidence for a difference in the degree of heritability in men and women, nor any evidence for genetic factors operating in one gender but not the other. This last conclusion was particularly aided by analyses of data from opposite-sex twin pairs, a type of analysis not previously reported. Using the same subject sample, these researchers have more recently demonstrated that childhood conduct disorder is significantly associated with risk for adult alcohol dependence in both men and women, with genetic factors accounting for most of the association in both genders. These findings further emphasize the similarities in factors leading to alcoholism in men and women and suggest either that there are common genetic risk factors for conduct disorder and alcoholism in both genders, or that conduct disorder is itself a genetic risk factor for alcoholism. Since the subject sample for these studies came from the general population and because most of the alcoholics contained therein were relatively mildly affected, it is possible that the conclusions of these studies might not apply to very severely affected alcoholics, such as those identified from treatment centers.

Children's Drinking Behavior Is Primarily Genetic

Since individuals who eventually become alcoholic typically begin experimenting with alcohol use during adolescence and then proceed through stages of increasingly heavy use until they become addicted, investigators have long been interested in factors influencing initiation of alcohol use during adolescence. The notion that adolescents learn to use alcohol by modeling the alcohol use of their parents is an old one. Investigators tested this notion in a sample of 1,396 Dutch families, each consisting of a pair of adolescent twins and their parents. The twins' alcohol use resembled that of their parents to some extent. For 17-year-olds, this resemblance could best be explained by genetic similarity of children to their parents, rather than by children modeling their parents' drinking behavior. For 15- to 16-year-olds, while the resemblance of the children's drinking to that of their parents was explained principally by some aspect of the familial environment, the parents' drinking behavior itself accounted for, at best, only a small part of this resemblance. It appears from this study that children's drinking behavior is influenced primarily by genetic factors and by environmental factors other than their parents' alcohol use. This conclusion is consistent with findings from previous studies demonstrating strong peer influences on adolescent alcohol use. . . .

Identifying genes influencing predisposition to alcoholism is of critical importance for improving prevention and treatment of alcoholism for two principal reasons. First, it will permit identification of the proteins the genes encode and elucidation of the physiologic pathways in which these proteins function. Every step of every such pathway represents a potential target for prevention or intervention, for example, by design of an appropriately targeted drug. Second, knowledge of the genes influencing predisposition to alcoholism will permit better design of studies to elucidate environmental influences on alcoholism by permitting control of variation at the relevant genes in the subject sample, thereby reducing confusion about whether observed differences between experimental and control subjects are due to environmental or genetic influences.

While twin/family studies . . . can provide information about the genetic architecture of alcoholism and the relationship between genetic influences on alcoholism and other traits, they do not permit the identification of the specific genes influencing predisposition to alcoholism. Current efforts to identify such genes rely on genetic linkage and association studies. Such studies have received enormous impetus in recent years from the mapping of large numbers of human genetic markers—recognizable sites along chromosomal deoxyribonucleic acid (DNA) that act as signposts for researchers—and genes under the Human Genome Project, which is supported by the National Institutes of Health and the U.S. Department of Energy, and from the development of more sophisticated statistical methods for analyzing gene mapping data.

Linkage Studies Identify Genetic Markers

Genetic linkage studies can be designed in either of two principal ways. In the first design, investigators track the inheritance of the disease, along with that of genetic markers spanning the entire genome, through multigenerational families affected by the disease. Various complex statistical analyses permit the determination of which markers are co-transmitted with the disease. In the second design, investigators measure the degree of sharing of different marker alleles by members of pairs of siblings (or other relatives) affected by the disease. On average, simply by chance, siblings are expected to share half of the alleles of most of their genes. However, two siblings affected by the same disease will show more frequent sharing of alleles of markers close to genes affecting predisposition to, or progress of, the disease. Under either design, markers shown to be genetically linked to a disease—that is, inherited with the disease more frequently than would be expected by chance—define a chromosomal region(s) likely to contain a gene(s) influencing the disease. The advantage of this approach to gene discovery is that a sufficiently comprehensive marker map, such as that now being assembled by the Human Genome Project, permits an unbiased search of the entire genome without requiring any prior physiologic hypothesis about which genes might influence the disease. Linkage studies work best for finding genes when the disease under study is influenced by a relatively small number of genes, each exerting a relatively large effect.

The results of the first two systematic searches of the entire human genome (termed "genome scans") for genes influencing predisposition to alcoholism have recently been published. The first study, by the Collaborative Study on Genetics of Alcoholism (COGA), a National Institute on Alcohol Abuse and Alcoholism (NIAAA)-supported consortium of investigators at six centers across the United States, reported results from a primarily Caucasian-American sample of 987 individuals from 105 families. In order to reduce errors in classification of subjects as alcoholic or non-alcoholic, the study defined alcohol-dependent individuals as those meeting two independent criteria for alcoholism: the DSM-IIIR criteria for alcohol dependence, and the Feighner criteria at the definite level. This study found suggestive evidence for genes influencing susceptibility to alcoholism on chromosomes 1 and 7 as well as weaker evidence for a gene on chromosome 2. It also reported modest evidence for a gene reducing the risk for alcoholism on chromosome 4. An independent genome scan, based on 152 subjects from a Southwestern American Indian tribe, has been reported by investigators in NIAAA's own research laboratories. With use of the DSM-IIIR definition of alcohol dependence, this study reported suggestive evidence for a gene influencing susceptibility to alcoholism on chromosome 11 as well as suggestive evidence for a protective gene on chromosome 4 in approximately the same region implicated by the COGA study.

A Protective Gene Exists in Diverse Groups

Rather than identifying specific genes, these studies have implicated certain chromosomal regions as containing genes influencing susceptibility to alcoholism. Each implicated region contains hundreds of genes, and determination of precisely which genes located therein influence alcoholism will require higher resolution mapping studies in the future. It is not surprising that the two studies implicated different chromosomal regions because (1) American Indians and Caucasian-Americans (of European descent) have different genetic histories and therefore contain different genetic variation, and (2) the physiologic mechanisms leading to alcoholism in American Indians may be different from those in Caucasians. In view of these differences between the two subject populations, it is of interest that both studies found some evidence for a protective gene in the same region of chromosome 4. Plausible candidates for this gene in this region are *ADH2* and *ADH3*, which encode alcohol dehydrogenases and for which some alleles have been shown to reduce susceptibility to alcoholism in Asian populations, and *GABARBI*, which encodes a subunit of a receptor for the major brain inhibitory neurotransmitter gamma-aminobutyric acid (GABA). The function of this receptor is stimulated by alcohol, possibly accounting for alcohol's sedating and motor-discoordinating effects. Long-term consumption of alcohol alters the brain distribution and function of this receptor, possibly playing a role in the development of alcohol dependence. Further studies will be required to determine whether any of these candidates is actually the gene inferred by both linkage studies to be responsible for protection from alcohol dependence.

The Location of Specific Genes Is Uncertain

The investigators responsible for both linkage studies have deliberately described their findings as suggestive rather than definitive. They exercise such caution because the observed sibling allele-sharing patterns (from which they have inferred the locations of the genes) deviate significantly from randomness but not so much so that one can be absolutely certain that the inferred genes are real. Certainty about the locations of the genes will require replication of the results of these studies in independent subject samples. Such studies are now under way. While these first two genome scans have not definitively identified genes influencing predisposition to alcoholism, they nonetheless represent a major step toward that goal. In the intermediate term, further progress will depend on the development of more sophisticated statistical methods that are capable of simultaneously analyzing data not only on alcoholism itself but also on a number of psychological and physiologic traits, such as temperament, sensitivity to alcohol, and various kinds of brain waves that may represent additional dimensions of the disease. These additional dimensions may ultimately constitute essential elements of biologically valid definitions of alcoholism, which will be a natural prerequisite for gene identification. Help in initial localization of disease genes will also come from new statistical methods for analyzing the effects of multiple genes simultaneously rather than one at a time, as most current methods do. Precise gene identification will depend ultimately on the development of a complete gene map of the human genome. It also will depend on use of genetic association studies . . . that test the association of alcoholism with specific alleles of genes lying within chromosomal regions identified by these and other linkage studies. . . .

Improved Treatment and Prevention Is the Goal

The greatest value expected to accrue from genetic studies toward the improvement of treatment and prevention of alcoholism will come from identification of the predisposing genes and the proteins they encode. . . .

Further progress toward precise identification of genes influencing predisposition to alcoholism will depend on the development of improved tools for the gene-discovery enterprise. Foremost among these tools will be more sophisticated statistical methods, a complete human gene map, and a catalogue of the major human genetic polymorphisms. Once genes influencing predisposition to alcoholism have been identified, a major new challenge confronting genetic epidemiologists will be to understand how such genes (many of which will have been discovered in families specially selected to be densely affected by alcoholism) interact with environmental factors to influence the development of alcoholism in the general population.

4

"Most claims linking emotional disorders and behaviors to genes are statistical in nature. . . . These calculations are . . . insufficient for deciding that alcoholism . . . is inherited."

The Genetic Influence on Alcoholism Is Exaggerated

Stanton Peele and Richard DeGrandpre

While many people would like to believe that alcoholism is genetic and therefore beyond individual control, in the following viewpoint Stanton Peele and Richard DeGrandpre contend that there is little scientific proof for that argument. They argue that the search for a genetic basis for alcoholism is part of a larger trend toward blaming everything on genetics and insisting that no one is personally responsible for their actions. The authors point out that when people believe that their personality and other traits are genetically determined at birth, they are conveniently absolved from having to behave themselves and conform to laws. Stanton Peele is a psychologist and researcher specializing in drug and alcohol addiction. Richard DeGrandpre is a visiting professor of psychology at Saint Michael's College in Colchester, Vermont.

As you read, consider the following questions:

1. According to Peele and DeGrandpre, how many pairs of chromosomes do human beings have?
2. In the authors' opinion, what is the most plausible model for any genetic involvement in alcoholism?

Stanton Peele and Richard DeGrandpre, "My Genes Made Me Do It," *Psychology Today*, July/August 1995. Copyright © 2003 by The Stanton Peele Addiction. Reproduced by permission.

Just about every week now, we read new headlines about the genetic basis for breast cancer, homosexuality, intelligence, or obesity. In previous years, these stories were about the genes for alcoholism, schizophrenia, and manic depression. Such news stories may lead us to believe our lives are being revolutionized by genetic discoveries. We may be on the verge of reversing and eliminating mental illness, for example. In addition, many believe, we can identify the causes of criminality, personality, and other basic human foibles and traits.

But these hopes, it turns out, are based on faulty assumptions about genes and behavior. Although genetic research wears the mantle of science, most of the headlines are more hype than reality. Many discoveries loudly touted to the public have been quietly refuted by further research. Other scientifically valid discoveries—like the gene for breast cancer—have nonetheless fallen short of initial claims. . . .

The public is hard pressed to evaluate which traits are genetically inspired based on the validity of scientific research. In many cases, people are motivated to accept research claims by the hope of finding solutions for frightening problems, like breast cancer, that our society has failed to solve. At a personal level, people wonder about how much actual choice they have in their lives. Accepting genetic causes for their traits can relieve guilt about behavior they want to change, but can't.

These psychological forces influence how we view mental illnesses like schizophrenia and depression, social problems like criminality, and personal maladies like obesity and bulimia. All have grown unabated in recent decades. Efforts made to combat them, at growing expense, have made little or no visible progress. The public wants to hear that science can help, while scientists want to prove that they have remedies for problems that eat away at our individual and social well-being.

Meanwhile, genetic claims are being made for a host of ordinary and abnormal behaviors, from addiction to shyness and even to political views and divorce. If who we are is determined from conception, then our efforts to change or to influence our children may be futile. There may also be no basis for insisting that people behave themselves and conform to laws. Thus, the revolution in thinking about genes has monumental consequences for how we view ourselves as human beings.

The Human Genome Project

Today scientists are mapping the entire genome—the DNA contained in the 23 pairs of human chromosomes. This enterprise is monumental. The chromosomes of each person contain 3 billion permutations of four chemical bases arrayed in two interlocking strands. This DNA may be divided into between 50,000 and 100,000 genes. But the same DNA can function in more than one gene, making the concept of individual genes something of a convenient fiction. The mystery of how these genes, and the chemistry underlying them, cause specific traits and diseases is a convoluted one.

The Human Genome Project has, and will continue to, advance our understanding of genes and suggest preventive and therapeutic strategies for many diseases. Some diseases, like Huntington's, have been linked to a single gene. But the search for single genes for complex human traits, like sexual orientation or antisocial behavior, or mental disorders like schizophrenia or depression, is seriously misguided.

Most claims linking emotional disorders and behaviors to genes are *statistical* in nature. For example, differences in the correlations in traits between identical twins (who inherit identical genes) and fraternal twins (who have half their genes in common) are examined with the goal of separating the role of environment from that of genes. But this goal is elusive. Research finds that identical twins are treated more alike than fraternal twins. These calculations are therefore insufficient for deciding that alcoholism or manic-depression is inherited, let alone television viewing, conservatism, and other basic, everyday traits for which such claims have been made.

In the late 1980s, genes for schizophrenia and manic-depression were identified with great fanfare by teams of geneticists. Both claims have now been definitively disproven. Yet, while the original announcements were heralded on TV news programs and front pages of newspapers around the country, most people are unaware of the refutations. . . .

Genes and Behavior

Understanding the role of our genetic inheritance requires that we know how genes express themselves. One popular conception is of genes as templates stamping out each human trait whole cloth. In fact, genes operate by instructing the developing organism to produce sequences of biochemical compounds.

In some cases, a single, dominant gene *does* largely determine a given trait. Eye color and Huntington's disease are classic examples of such Mendelian traits (named after the Austrian monk, Gregor Mendel, who studied peas). But the problem for behavioral genetics is that complex human attitudes and behavior—and even most diseases—are not determined by single genes.

Moreover, even at the cellular level, environment affects the activity of genes. Most active genetic material does not code for any kind of trait. Instead it regulates the speed and direction of the expression of other genes; i.e., it modulates the unfolding of the genome. Such regulatory DNA reacts to conditions inside and outside the womb, stimulating different rates of biochemical activity and cellular growth. Rather than forming a rigid template for each of us, genes themselves form part of a lifelong give-and-take process with the environment.

The inextricable interplay between genes and environment is evident in disorders like alcoholism, anorexia, or overeating that are characterized by abnormal behaviors. Scientists spiritedly debate whether such syndromes are more or less biologically driven. If they are mainly biological—rather than psychological, social, and cultural—then there may be a genetic basis for them.

Therefore, there was considerable interest in the announcement of the discovery of an "alcoholism gene" in 1990. Kenneth Blum, of the University of Texas, and Ernest Noble, of the University of California, found an allele of the dopamine receptor gene in 70 percent of a group of alcoholics but in only 20 percent of a non-alcoholic group. (An allele is one variation at a gene site.)

The Blum-Noble discovery was broadcast around the country after being published in the *Journal of the American*

Medical Association and touted by the AMA on its satellite news service. But, in a 1993 *JAMA* article, Joel Gelernter of Yale and his colleagues surveyed all the studies that examined this allele and alcoholism. Discounting Blum and Noble's research, the combined results were that 18 percent of nonalcoholics, 18 percent of problem drinkers, and 18 percent of severe alcoholics *all* had the allele. There was simply no link between this gene and alcoholism!

Blum and Noble have developed a test for the alcoholism gene. But, since their own data indicate that the majority of people who have the target allele are not alcoholics, it would be foolhardy to tell those who test positive that they have an "alcoholism gene."

There Is No Genetic Marker for Alcoholism

While the application of the medical disease model to addictions was developed to "remove the stigma from these behaviors", there is no genetic marker for alcoholism or drug addiction. Still, the misconception that these behaviors are linked to a genetic vulnerability is aired repeatedly by the media, in the absence of evidence. The rationale for using the disease model to describe addiction even though it is intellectually dishonest is that medical treatment is effective.

Ilana Mercer, *Calgary Herald*, June 22, 2000.

The dubious state of Blum and Noble's work does not disprove that a gene—or set of genes—could trigger alcoholism. But scientists already know that people do not inherit loss-of-control drinking whole cloth. Consider that alcoholics do not drink uncontrollably when they are unaware that they are drinking alcohol—if it is disguised in a flavored drink, for example.

A more plausible model is that genes affect how people experience alcohol. Perhaps drinking is more rewarding for alcoholics. Perhaps some people's neurotransmitters are more activated by alcohol. But although genes can influence reactions to alcohol, they cannot explain why some people continue drinking to the point of destroying their lives. Most people find orgasms rewarding, but hardly any engage in sex uncontrollably. Rather, they balance their sexual urges against other forces in their lives.

Jerome Kagan, a Harvard developmental psychologist, was speaking about more than genes when he noted, "we also inherit the human capacity for restraint."

Public interest was aroused by the 1995 announcement by Rockefeller University geneticist Jeffrey Friedman of a genetic mutation in obese mice. The researchers believe this gene influences development of a hormone that tells the organism how fat or full it is. Those with the mutation may not sense when they have achieved satiety or if they have sufficient fatty tissue, and thus can't tell when to stop eating. . . .

Actually, behavior geneticists believe that less than half of total weight variation is programmed in the genes, while height is almost entirely genetically determined. Whatever role genes play, America is getting fatter. A survey by the Centers for Disease Control found that obesity has increased significantly over the last 10 years. Such rapid change underlines the role of environmental factors, like the abundance of rich foods, in America's overeating. Complimenting this finding, the Centers have found that teens are far less physically active than they were even a decade ago. . . .

The case of obesity—along with schizophrenia, depression, and alcoholism—raises a striking paradox. At the same time that we now view them as diseases that should be treated medically, their prevalence is growing precipitously. The very reliance on drugs and other medical treatments has created a cultural milieu that seeks external solutions for these problems. Relying on external solutions may itself be exacerbating matters; it may be teaching us a helplessness that is at the root of many of our problems. Instead of reducing our problems, this seems to have fueled their growth. . . .

Many Genes May Be Involved in a Single Trait

In 1993, the gene that determines the occurrence of Huntington's disease—an irreversible degeneration of the nervous system—was discovered. In 1994, a gene was identified that leads to some cases of breast cancer. Utilizing these discoveries, however, is proving more difficult than anticipated.

Finding a gene for breast cancer was cause for elation. But of all the women with breast cancer, only a tenth have family histories of the disease. Furthermore, only half of this group has a mutation in the gene. Scientists also hoped that breast cancer victims without family histories would show irregularities at this same site on the DNA. But only a small minority do. . . .

These difficulties with a disease created by an individual gene show the monumental complexity involved in unraveling how genes determine complex human traits.

When a distinct gene is not involved, linking genes to traits may well be an absurdity. Any possible link between genes and traits is exponentially more complex with elaborate behavior patterns like overdrinking, personality characteristics like shyness or aggressiveness, or social attitudes such as political conservatism and religiousness. Many genes might be involved in all such traits. More importantly, it is impossible to separate the contributions environment and DNA make to attitudes and behaviors. . . .

The research discussed so far searches for genes implicated in specific problems. But research relating behavior and genetics rarely involves actual examination of the genome. Instead, psychologists, psychiatrists and other non-geneticists calculate a heritability statistic by comparing the similarities in behaviors among different sets of relatives. This statistic expresses the old nature-nurture division by presenting the percentage of a trait due to genetic inheritance versus the percentage due to environmental causes.

Such research purports to show a substantial genetic component to alcoholism. For example, some studies have compared the incidence of alcoholism in adopted children with that of their adoptive parents and with their natural parents. When the similarities are greater between the offspring and absent biologic parents, the trait is thought to be highly heritable.

But children are often adopted by relatives or people from the same social background as the parents. The very social factors related to placement of a child—particularly ethnicity and social class—are also related to drinking problems, for example, thus confusing efforts to separate nature and nurture. A team led by University of California sociologist Kaye Fillmore incorporated social data on adoptive families in the reanalysis of two studies claiming a large genetic inheritance for alcoholism. Fillmore found that the educational and economic level of the receiving families had the greater influence, statistically erasing the genetic contribution from the biological parents. . . .

Heritability figures in fact vary widely from study to study. Matthew McGue and his colleagues at the University of Minnesota calculated a 0 heritability of alcoholism in women, while at the same time a team led by Kenneth Kendler at Virginia Medical College calculated a 60 percent heritability with a different group of female twins! One problem is that the number of female alcoholic twins is small, which is true of most abnormal conditions we study. As a result, the high heritability figure Kendler et al. found would be reduced to nothing with a shift in the diagnoses of as few as four twins in their study.

Shifting definitions also contribute to variations in the heritability measured for alcoholism. Alcoholism may be defined as any drinking problems, or only physiological problems such as DTs, or various combinations of criteria. These variations in methodology explain why heritability figures for alcoholism in different studies vary from 0 to almost 100 percent. . . .

The Inheritance of Everyday Psychological Traits

By assigning a simple percentage to something very complex and poorly understood, behavior geneticists turn heritability into a clear-cut measurement. Behavior geneticists have employed these same statistical techniques with ordinary behaviors and attitudes. The resulting list of traits for which heritability has been calculated extends from such well known areas as intelligence, depression, and shyness to such surprising ones as television viewing, divorce, and attitudes like racial prejudice and political conservatism.

Such heritability figures may seem quite remarkable, even incredible. Behavior geneticists report that half of the basis of divorce, bulimia and attitudes about punishing criminals is biologically inherited, comparable to or higher than the figures calculated for depression, obesity, and anxiety. Almost any trait seemingly yields a minimum heritability figure around 30 percent. The heritability index acts like a scale that reads 30 pounds when empty and adds 30 pounds to everything placed on it!

Believing that basic traits are largely predetermined at birth could have tremendous implications for our self-conceptions and public policies. Not long ago, an announcement for a government conference, for example, suggested that violence could be prevented by treating with drugs children with certain genetic profiles. Or, parents of children with an alcoholic heritage may tell the children never to drink because they're destined to be alcoholics. But such children, in expecting to become violent or drink excessively, may enact a self-fulfilling prophecy. Indeed, this is known to be the case. People who believe they are alcoholic drink more when told a beverage contains alcohol—even if it doesn't.

Believing the heritability figures developed by behavioral geneticists leads to an important conclusion: Most people must then be overestimating how much daily impact they have on important areas of children's development. Why ask Junior to turn off the TV set if television viewing is inherited, as some claim? What, exactly, can parents accomplish if traits such as prejudice are largely inherited? It would not seem to matter what values we attempt to convey to our children. Likewise, if violence is mostly inbred, then it doesn't make much sense to try to teach our kids to behave properly.

View from the Genome

The vision of humanity generated by statistical research on behavior genetics seems to enhance the passivity and fatalism many people are already saddled with. Yet evidence gathered by psychologist Martin Seligman and others indicates that "learned helplessness"—or believing one cannot influence one's destiny—is a major factor in depression. The opposite state of mind occurs when people believe they control what happens to them. Called self-efficacy, it is a major contributor to psychological well-being and successful functioning.

Is there a connection between the increase in depression and other emotional disorders in 20th-century America and our outlook as a society? If so, then the growing belief that our behavior is not ours to determine could have extremely negative consequences. As well as attacking our own sense of personal self-determination, it may make us less able to disapprove of the misbehavior of others. After all, if people are born to be alcoholic or violent, how can they be punished when they translate these dispositions into action . . . ?

How much freedom each person has to develop returns us to the issue of whether nature and nurture can be separated. Thinking of traits as being either genetically or environmentally caused cripples our understanding of human development. As [Jerome] Kagan puts it, "To ask what proportion of personality is genetic rather than environmental is like asking what proportion of a blizzard is due to cold temperature rather than humidity."

A more accurate model is one in which chains of events split into further layers of possible paths. Let's return to alcoholism. Drinking produces greater mood change for some people. Those who find alcohol to serve a strong palliative function will be more likely to use it to calm themselves. For example, if they are highly anxious, alcohol may tranquilize them. But even this tranquilizing effect, we should recognize, is strongly influenced by social learning.

Among drinkers who are potentially vulnerable to alcohol's addictive effects, most will nonetheless find alternatives to drinking to deal with anxiety. Perhaps their social group disapproves of excessive drinking, or their own values strongly rule out drunkenness. Thus, although people who find alcohol redresses their anxiety are more likely to drink addictively than others, they are not programmed to do so. . . .

The goal of determining what proportion of behavior is genetic and environmental will always elude us. Our personalities and destinies don't evolve in this straightforward manner. Behavioral genetics actually shows us how the statistical plumbing of the human spirit has reached its limits. Claims that our genes cause our problems, our misbehavior, even our personalities are more a mirror of our culture's attitudes than a window for human understanding and change.

"Youth saw more beer and ale advertising in 2001 than they saw advertising for gum, or cookies and crackers, or sneakers."

Alcohol Advertising Targeted to Youth Causes Abuse

Center on Alcohol Marketing and Youth

While the alcohol industry claims that it does not target underage drinkers, its voluntary guidelines are so lax that it allows advertising on programs with a majority of young people in the viewing audience, researchers for the Center on Alcohol Marketing and Youth argue in the following viewpoint. They contend that exposure to an excessive amount of advertising that glamorizes drinking or portrays abusive drinking behavior in a positive way encourages young people to start drinking, often abusively, at an early age. The Center on Alcohol Marketing and Youth at Georgetown University monitors the effect of the marketing practices of the alcohol industry on American youth.

As you read, consider the following questions:
1. According to the center, what percentage of the national television population is between twelve and twenty?
2. Name one reason why society should be concerned about alcohol advertising to youth, in the researchers' opinion.
3. In 2001 how many alcohol ads were seen by more youth than adults, as cited by the authors?

C oncern about how much television alcohol advertising reaches underage youth and how the advertising influences their attitudes and decisions about alcohol use has been widespread for many years. Lacking in the policy debate has been solid, reliable information about the extent of youth exposure to television alcohol advertising. To address this critical gap, the Center on Alcohol Marketing and Youth commissioned Virtual Media Resources, a media planning and research firm in Natick, Massachusetts, to analyze television alcohol advertising in 2001, using the same data and methodology as professional media planners.

In auditing 208,909 alcohol ad placements on television in 2001, the Center on Alcohol Marketing and Youth finds the following:

1. The alcohol industry's voluntary guidelines for ad placements on television are so lax that they allow the substantial exposure of youth to alcoholic beverage advertising, including advertising on programs with disproportionate numbers of young people in the viewing audience.

2. Even when adults were more likely to see television alcohol advertising than youth, in many instances youth saw almost as much television alcohol advertising as the adults.

3. Because of the placement of the commercials, almost a quarter of alcohol advertising on television in 2001 was more likely to be seen by youth than adults.

The Standard for Measuring Youth Exposure

Youth are only 15% of the national television viewing population (age 12 and over) and represent only 15.6% of the general U.S. population, age 12 and up. When advertising is placed on programs where the youth viewing audience is more than 15%, young people are more likely to see that advertising than adults. In 1999, the Federal Trade Commission pointed out that a few alcohol companies restricted their television ad placements to programming where the youth audience was 30%, 25%, or less, and called these "best practices." Noting that "30 percent of the U.S. population is under the age of 21, and only ten percent is age 11 to 17," the

FTC concluded that the alcohol industry's voluntary guidelines providing for a 50% threshold for underage youth in the audience "permits placement of ads on programs where the underage audience far exceeds its representation in the population."

The FTC's recommendations notwithstanding, the voluntary advertising codes of the Beer Institute and the Distilled Spirits Council of the United States (DISCUS) suggest that alcohol advertisers refrain from airing their commercials on programs where young people are the majority of the viewing audience. Using a base of viewers age 12 and older, only one percent of all network and cable television programs in 2001 (187 out of 14,359) had an underage audience that was more than 50%. Thus the brewers' and distillers' voluntary codes leave 99% of the television landscape permissible for alcohol advertising.

Beer and Ale Ads Are Seen Most in TV Alcohol Advertising

Even when alcohol advertising was placed on programming with 15% or less youth in the viewing audience, youth exposure to alcohol advertising on television in 2001 was substantial and significant. In 2001 youth saw two beer and ale ads for every three seen by an adult. Given the high volume of beer and ale advertising to adults, this ratio translates into a high volume of youth exposure, representing more than 200 commercial exposures for the average youth, and far more exposures for those youth who are frequent viewers of television. Beer and ale advertising is by far the dominant television alcohol advertising. Of the $811.2 million in television advertising (208,909 ads) analyzed in this study, beer and ale accounted for 86% of the ad spending.

Four beer and ale brands accounted for more than 50% of the total spending of television advertising analyzed: Coors Light, $114 million; Budweiser, $108 million; Miller Lite, $95.8 million; and Bud Light, $88.7 million.

- Youth saw more than two Coors Light ads for every three seen by an adult.
- Youth saw more than one Budweiser ad for every two seen by an adult.

- Youth saw almost three Miller Lite ads for every four seen by an adult.
- Youth saw more than one Bud Light ad for every two seen by an adult.

Another way to assess the volume of alcohol advertising seen by youth is to compare it to product categories often considered youth-oriented. In this light, youth saw more beer and ale ads on television in 2001 than they saw ads for other product categories such as fruit juices and fruit-flavored drinks; or gum; or skin care products; or cookies and crackers; or chips, nuts, popcorn and pretzels; or sneakers; or non-carbonated soft drinks; or sportswear jeans.

Overall in 2001, alcohol advertising reached 89% of the youth audience, who on average saw 245 alcohol ads. But the 30% of youth who were most likely to see alcohol advertising on TV saw at least 780 ads.

Youth Overexposed to Television Alcohol Advertising

Almost a quarter of the television alcohol advertising in 2001—51,084 ads—was delivered more effectively to youth than to adults. This means the advertising was placed on programs where the youth audience was higher than the percentage of youth in the television viewing population. That percentage is 15% nationally and varies slightly from market to market. By placing advertising on programs where the composition of the youth audience is higher than average, the youth audience is in effect "overexposed" to the advertising and is more likely to have seen it than the adult audience.

The alcohol industry placed these 51,084 ads on television in 2001 at a cost of $119 million. Ten beer and "malternative" (also known as "low alcohol refresher") brands accounted for $92 million of this spending:

- Miller Lite, $18.5 million
- Heineken, $16.2 million
- Coors Light, $13.6 million
- Miller Genuine Draft, $10.5 million
- Budweiser, $8.4 million
- Bud Light, $7.3 million
- Corona Extra, $5.6 million

- Smirnoff Ice, $4.8 million
- Foster's, $3.8 million
- Mike's Hard Lemonade, $3.5 million

The ads were broadcast on shows ranging from sports programs like *Sports Center* and the NBA and Stanley Cup playoffs, to drama programs like *Dark Angel* and *X-Files*, variety programs like *MADtv* and *Saturday Night Live*, situation comedies like *That '70s Show* and *Titus*, and talk shows like *Late Night with Conan O'Brien* and *The Daily Show*.

Five networks—WB, UPN, Comedy Central, BET and VH-1—routinely overexposed youth to alcohol advertising in 2001. Two types of programming—variety shows like *MADtv* on Fox and *Insomniac Music Theater* on VH-1, and music, video and entertainment shows like *Midnight Love* on BET and *Top 10 Countdown* on VH-1—also overexposed youth to alcohol advertising in 2001. For instance, youth had 110% greater exposure to alcohol advertising on Comedy Central than did legal-age adults. On variety shows, youth had 26% greater exposure to alcohol advertising than did legal-age adults.

Why Alcohol Advertising Is a Cause for Concern

Underage drinking in the United States is marked by abuse. For 15- to 17-year-olds, 25% report being current drinkers, and 65% of those current drinkers report having had five or more drinks on at least one occasion: By the time they are 18 to 20 years old, 48% report being current drinkers, and 71% of those drinkers report having had five or more drinks on at least one occasion. The vast majority of the alcohol consumed by young people is for the purposes of intoxication: 92% of the alcohol drunk by 12- to 14-year-olds and 96% of the consumption by 15- to 17-year-olds and 18- to 20-year-olds is done when drinkers are having five or more drinks at one time. More than a thousand young drivers died in crashes after drinking in 2001. While the total number of young drivers dying in motor vehicle crashes fell from 1999 to 2001, alcohol-related fatalities in this group are rising.

In 2002, the Henry J. Kaiser Family Foundation and The National Center on Addiction and Substance Abuse at Columbia University surveyed youth about drinking and risky sexual behavior. Among 15- to 17-year-olds, 29% of the respondents said alcohol or drugs had influenced their decision to engage in sexual activity. Almost a quarter of the 15- to 17-year-olds reported that they had done more sexually than planned because of alcohol or drug use. Slightly more than a quarter of this age group reported they were concerned about sexually transmitted diseases or pregnancy because of their alcohol or drug use.

Alcohol Advertising Promotes Myths

The alcohol industry spends over two billion dollars a year on advertising and promotion. Many of their ads falsely link alcohol with precisely those attributes and qualities—happiness, wealth, prestige, sophistication, success, maturity, athletic ability, virility, creativity, sexual satisfaction, and others—that the abuse of alcohol diminishes and destroys. Such advertising promotes myths about alcohol that contribute to both individual and collective denial. Perhaps most insidiously, alcohol advertisers target alcoholics and heavy drinkers (their best customers, after all) with the promise that alcohol can be a substitute for human relationships and can thus assuage the loneliness that is at the heart of all addictions. Alcohol advertising also encourages young people to believe that drinking heavily is a route to freedom.

Jean Kilbourne, 128th Annual Meeting of the American Public Health Association, November 13, 2000.

The voluntary advertising guidelines of the alcohol industry explicitly recognize the dangers of advertising that glamorizes or portrays abusive drinking behavior or sexual themes. For instance, the Beer Industry's voluntary code states: "Beer advertising and marketing materials should not depict situations where beer is being consumed excessively, in an irresponsible way, or in any way illegally." It goes on to state: "Beer advertising and marketing materials should not portray sexual passion, promiscuity or any other amorous activities as a result of consuming beer." The DISCUS advertising guidelines contain similar admonitions to its members. For instance, "Distilled spirits advertising and marketing should portray distilled spirits and drinkers in a responsible manner. These materials should not show a distilled spirits product being consumed abusively or irresponsibly."

The Federal Trade Commission (FTC) has noted that "while many factors may influence an underage person's drinking decisions, including among other things parents, peers and media, there is reason to believe that advertising also plays a role." Research studies have found that exposure to and liking of alcohol advertisements affects young people's beliefs about drinking, intentions to drink, and actual drinking behavior. . . .

Industry Guidelines Are Not Strict Enough

The alcohol industry has adopted guidelines on advertising placement that purport to limit the exposure of youth to alcohol advertising on television while allowing the industry to market its products to legal-age adults.

In fact, the industry guidelines place a very small percentage of television programming off limits for alcohol ads. Using a base of viewers age 12 and older, only one percent of all network and cable television programs in 2001 (187 out of 14,359) have an underage audience that is more than 50%—the beer and distilled spirits industries' threshold for not advertising. Using a base of viewers age 2 and older, only six percent of all network and cable television programs in 2001 (888 out of 14,359) have an underage audience that is more than 50%.

As it was in 2001, even the 50% threshold was violated. The alcohol industry spent $1.8 million and placed 3,262 ads on programs where the underage audience was more than 50%.

More significantly, more than 51,000 alcohol ads were seen by a greater percentage of youth than adults in 2001. The industry spent $119 million on this advertising, and it represented nearly a quarter of the industry's television ad placements. Even when the alcohol industry placed ads on television that were seen by more adults than youth, underage youth were seeing a substantial amount of alcohol advertising. For instance, youth saw more beer and ale advertising in 2001 than they saw advertising for gum, or cookies and crackers, or sneakers. Often, youth were seeing two alcohol ads for every three seen by adults, or three alcohol ads for every four seen by adults.

Youth actually make up a smaller percentage of both the television viewing audience and the U.S. population in general than indicated by the alcohol industry guidelines. Youth are only 15% of the Nielsen television population (age 12 and over) and only 15.6% of the general population 12+. Furthermore, their presence in the audience actually viewing television only averages 10% overall.

Even following a 15% threshold would still have resulted in more than 22,000 television ads in 2001 where a greater percentage of youth than adults would have been exposed to the alcohol advertising. And a 15% threshold allows for the viewing of alcohol advertising by millions of underage youth in the case of major sporting events such as the Super Bowl or awards shows such as the Academy Awards. However, following this threshold would have provided more protection of youth than the current marketplace does.

In 1999, the Federal Trade Commission called upon the industry to adopt "best practices" on advertising placements. For television placements, the FTC pointed as a "best practice" to some companies adopting "a 70 to 75 percent legal-age audience for television placements."

This report shows that it is time for the FTC to review the alcohol industry's television advertising practices and to determine whether the "best practices" the Commission advocated in 1999 have been adopted and, more importantly, whether those practices indeed provide for adequate protection of the nation's youth from overexposure to alcohol advertising on television.

"Members of the [beer] industry comply with . . . voluntary advertising codes, which prohibit blatant appeals to young audiences and advertising in venues where most of the audience is under the legal drinking age."

Alcohol Advertising Targeted to Youth May Not Cause Abuse

International Center for Alcohol Policies

The alcoholic beverage industry practices effective voluntary self-regulation in concert with trade associations and federal agencies, the International Center for Alcohol Policies (ICAP) argues in the following viewpoint. The center further contends that the Federal Trade Commission (FTC) has concluded that the industry does not direct alcohol advertising to young audiences. Moreover, despite critics' claims that exposure to alcohol advertising could lead youths to abuse alcohol, there is no conclusive evidence that such advertising influences drinking beliefs. The International Center for Alcohol Policies, a nonprofit organization supported by eleven international beverage alcohol companies, is dedicated to reducing the abuse of alcohol worldwide.

As you read, consider the following questions:
1. According to the center, what are the two basic elements of self-regulation?
2. What was the conclusion of the Department of Health and Human Services regarding the effects of alcohol advertising on alcohol-related problems?

An important element of public policy is developing standards regarding how the private sector communicates information about their products. Ideally, advertising is meant to inform the public so that they can be aware of products and make informed choices among different products or brands. Advertising is, of course, also of benefit to businesses in assisting them to sell their products, which in most countries is a commercial right.

This issue of *ICAP* [*International Center for Alcohol Policies*] *Reports* will explore the concept of self-regulation in relation to the advertising of alcohol beverages. It will explore the elements of different codes and how they are applied in practice. It is recognized that advertising is one of several forms of commercial communication, including sponsorship, promotion and the Internet. . . .

Self-regulation is the process whereby industry actively participates in and is responsible for its own regulation. While this process varies widely from country to country, the foundation for advertising self-regulation is based on the principles embodied in the International Code of Advertising, issued by the International Chamber of Commerce. The Code states in its introduction that advertising should be legal, decent, honest and truthful, prepared with a sense of social responsibility to the consumer and society and with proper respect for the rules of fair competition. This is accomplished through rules and principles of best practice to which advertisers and the advertising industry agree to be bound.

The basic elements of self-regulation are two-fold: a code of practice or set of guiding principles governing the content of advertisements, and a process for the establishment, review and application of the code or principles. Impartiality is seen to be key to an effective code and public trust in it. . . .

There may be several self-regulatory bodies to which a given alcohol beverage company must adhere regarding commercial communications. . . .

Voluntary Advertising Codes Are the Key

The alcohol beverage industry in the United States has established separate voluntary advertising codes initiated by trade associations from each of the three sectors that make up the industry—beer, wine and distilled spirits. At the same time, the Federal Trade Commission (FTC) is responsible for enforcing efforts to stop "unfair or deceptive acts of practice" and recently was asked to review industry efforts to avoid promoting alcohol to underage consumers.

Generally, the three codes provide that alcohol advertising and marketing efforts should not be directed at or appeal to an audience that is primarily underage. In conducting their review, the FTC looked at issues such as advertising placement, advertising content, product placement, online advertising and college marketing, how each of these were implemented and what best practices emerged.

The Impact of Advertising on Young People

The impact of alcohol advertising on young people has received considerable attention. A substantial body of research has been devoted to the respective roles of family, peers, culture, social forces, media, and other significant factors in determining the decision by young people whether or not to drink. The most powerful factors in shaping beliefs and attitudes about drinking are parental and peer influence. Alcohol advertising, on the other hand, plays only a small role. In fact, there is no compelling evidence of a correlation between advertising and either drinking patterns among young people, or rates of abuse. It is likely that other forces, especially parental and peer influences, play a more significant role and that drinking patterns among young people are much more likely to be influenced by the prevailing culture around alcohol, than by advertising.

"Industry Views on Beverage Alcohol Advertising and Marketing with Special Reference to Young People," International Center for Alcohol Policies, 2002.

The FTC report concluded that "for the most part, members of the industry comply with the current standards set by the voluntary advertising codes, which prohibit blatant appeals to young audiences and advertising in venues where most of the audience is under the legal drinking age." The report also noted that many individual companies had their own internal standards that exceed code requirements.

Third-party review that would provide for an independent

assessment of complaints was one recommendation cited by the FTC to improve the codes still further. Several beverage alcohol companies support this recommendation in one form or another, but opinion about the need for this enhancement is divided. The best practices cited by the FTC include prohibiting ads with substantial underage appeal even if they also appeal to adults, and curbing on-campus and spring break sponsorships and advertising.

The three codes operated by the Beer Institute, the Distilled Spirits Council of the United States (DISCUS) and the Wine Institute have generally strengthened their provisions over the years. In 1997, DISCUS repealed one of its provisions which called for a ban on spirits advertising on television. This change put the DISCUS code in line with the codes of the Beer Institute and the Wine Institute on this issue. DISCUS argued that if beer and wine were allowed to advertise on television with certain restrictions, the spirits industry should be too. There was strong adverse reaction to ending the ban, which had been in place for 50 years. However, in the end, the response to this reaction was not to legislate, but for most major broadcast television networks to decline to accept spirits advertising. The spirits industry continues to strongly promote the expansion of their advertising over the broadcast media, though networks have yet to accept such advertising.

This example also illustrates that self-regulation is not simply incumbent upon the alcohol beverage industry to police itself. It acts in concert with the agencies responsible for advertising form and content as well as the media that carry the advertising. . . .

Research on the Effects of Advertising Is Not Conclusive

In recent years, public health advocates have called for strict regulation or elimination of alcohol advertising, and particular attention has been drawn to how alcohol advertising might affect young people. The argument that alcohol advertising is intended to create brand preference and not give cause for abuse by showing irresponsible consumption rings hollow among these critics, some of whom believe that advertising increases alcohol abuse and that self-regulation does little to prevent this.

The U.S. Department of Health and Human Services recently reviewed the evidence on the effects of alcohol advertising on alcohol consumption, alcohol-related problems and drinking-related beliefs and attitudes. Studies were drawn from seven diverse fields. The overall conclusion was that survey research on alcohol advertising and young people "consistently indicates small but significant connections between exposure to and awareness of alcohol advertising and drinking beliefs and behaviors." The report adds that taken as a whole, the survey studies provide some evidence that alcohol advertising may influence drinking beliefs but that this evidence is far from conclusive. "When all of the studies are considered, the results of research on the effects of alcohol advertising are mixed and not conclusive." The report states that with few exceptions, recent econometric research provides "very little consistent evidence that alcohol advertising influences per capita alcohol consumption, sales or problems."

Periodical Bibliography

The following articles have been selected to supplement the diverse views presented in this chapter.

Beer Institute	"Advertising Warning Legislation," Beer Institute Online, April 2003. www.beerinstitute.org.
Brown University Digest of Addiction Theory and Application	"Risk for Developing Alcoholism Linked to Genetic Characteristics," October 2000.
Free Republic	"Study: Kids Exposed to TV Beer Marketing," December 12, 2002. www.freerepublic.com.
John Gaffney	"New Alcohol Study Refuted by Industry," *Media Daily News*, December 12, 2002. www.mediapost.com.
Susan Greenfield	"Alcohol on the Brain: Myths and Mysteries," Alcohol in Moderation, May 14, 2002. www.aim-digest.com.
International Center for Alcohol Policies	"Industry Views on Beverage Alcohol Advertising and Marketing, with Special Reference to Young People," 2002. www.icap.org.
David H. Jernigan	"The Global Expansion of Alcohol Marketing: Illustrative Case Studies and Recommendations for Action," *Journal of Public Health Policy*, 1999.
Ilana Mercer	"Addictions Are About Behavior, Not Disease," *Calgary Herald*, June 22, 2000.
Modern Brewery Age	"Beer Industry Responds to CAMY Underage Drinking Report with New Stats," December 30, 2002.
National Highway Traffic Safety Administration	"Age of Drinking Onset and Unintentional Injury Involvement After Drinking," January 2001. www.nhtsa.gov.
Vanessa O'Connell and Christopher Lawton	"Anti-Alcohol Group Seeks Limits on TV Ads," *Wall Street Journal*, December 18, 2002.
Pain and Central Nervous System Week	"Researchers Track Gene Responsible for Alcohol Withdrawal," June 3, 2002.
University of Michigan and National Institute on Drug Abuse	"Monitoring the Future Survey," December 13, 2002. www.monitoringthefuture.org.
Paula J. Wart	"Just Like Dear Old Dad: Alcoholism May Be in the Genes," *Wellsource*, April 3, 2002.

CHAPTER 3

How Should Alcoholism Be Treated?

Chapter Preface

There are many treatment programs available for alcoholics—years of research have shown that no one program works for all alcohol abusers. Private psychotherapy or the use of medications such as Antabuse helps some people stop drinking. Many researchers believe that a combination of therapy and medication is the answer while other scientists are confident that some sort of genetic therapy will soon be available to help problem drinkers. The most common, although not necessarily the most effective, form of treatment is traditional twelve-step group recovery programs such as Alcoholics Anonymous (AA). Statistics show that most alcoholics try AA at some point, but few actually achieve sobriety in the program. In fact, there are many alcoholics who disagree vehemently with AA's philosophies and practices and have found non-faith-based self-help treatment programs more effective. Critics of twelve-step programs argue that there is no scientific basis for AA's definition of alcoholism as a disease. Further, they dislike AA's religious emphasis and insistence that only a higher power can help them stop drinking.

One such program, Rational Recovery, is an aggressive self-help program that does not depend on belief in a higher power but is based on individual responsibility, resiliency, self-reliance, and personal independence. The founder, Jack Trimpey, was an alcoholic who had tried to become sober using Alcoholics Anonymous's program. Angered and disillusioned by AA's religious underpinnings and the organization's demand that he recognize his alcoholism as a disease over which he had no control, Trimpey became determined to conquer his drinking problem by himself. He maintains, "Very few who actually recover from substance addictions do it by attending meetings, entering treatment centers, or getting counseling." A trained social worker, he drew on his knowledge of human behavior to develop a rational approach to his own recovery from alcoholism and, in 1986, he founded the Rational Recovery program. According to Trimpey, Rational Recovery is a planned abstinence program that is based on what he calls the Addictive Voice Recognition Technique (AVRT). He contends that "AVRT is a description of the awesome potential of addicted people to take personal responsibility for lifetime abstinence and to become normal, healthy, independent people who simply never drink or use other drugs." Rational Recovery has no members and holds no meetings; AVRT information can be obtained free over the Internet or by purchasing Trimpey's books.

Accepting that alcoholism is not a disease and acknowledging that considering it so is "nothing more than a doctor's excuse for one's past, present, and future drinking," is key to Trimpey's Rational Recovery program. Like many other experts who reject the disease concept of alcoholism, Trimpey considers it a ploy that alcoholics use to avoid being held accountable for their intentional misbehavior. Moreover, he insists that the addiction industry (treatment providers, recovery groups such as AA, and treatment centers) has a vested interest in maintaining the illusion that alcoholism is a disease. Supported by the court system and social service agencies, the addiction industry profits financially from the endless recovery/relapse cycles of alcoholics who are made to believe that they have a chronic disease. Trimpey contends that alcoholics do not need to be told that they are sick or that they need support from a recovery group to stop drinking permanently—they only need to learn the thinking skills on which Rational Recovery is based.

Rational Recovery's insistence that alcoholism is a question of personal responsibility and self-reliance stands in sharp contrast to the more publicized group recovery programs' contentions that alcoholics have a disease over which they are powerless. Authors in the following chapter debate the effectiveness of these and other forms of treatment for alcoholism.

"Failure to understand alcoholism as a chronic disease has contributed to a perception that treatment is ineffective, and that people don't quit drinking because they are weak-willed."

Alcoholism Should Be Treated as a Disease

Jeffrey Hon

In the following viewpoint Jeffrey Hon argues that alcoholism is a chronic disease that can be clinically diagnosed and treated, much like asthma, diabetes, or high blood pressure. He contends, therefore, that it should not be socially stigmatized but treated as a health issue with regard to treatment plans and insurance coverage. Treating alcoholism as a social problem only is not sound public health policy, Hon maintains. Jeffrey Hon is a researcher for Ensuring Solutions to Alcohol Problems, a research-based organization that helps increase access to alcohol treatment, at the George Washington University Medical Center.

As you read, consider the following questions:

1. According to Jeffrey Hon, how many Americans suffer from alcoholism?
2. In what respects does alcoholism strongly resemble other chronic diseases such as asthma, diabetes, and high blood pressure, in Hon's opinion?
3. Hon argues that once people are motivated to seek treatment, they may not be able to get it. Why?

Nearly 14 million Americans have serious problems because of their drinking, including eight million men
and women who suffer from alcoholism, a chronic disease.
Alcoholism can be clinically diagnosed and people with the
disease typically experience many additional alcohol-related
medical complications. Research demonstrates that treatment can save lives, restore families, reduce health care
costs, increase productivity in the workplace and make our
communities safer.

Yet while most Americans believe that alcoholism is a disease, the nation continues to deal with it more often as a social problem than a health issue. One reason is stigma, the
social disapproval that confronts people with addiction to
any drug. Stigma discourages people who are dependent on
alcohol from seeking medical attention and prevents the nation from accepting that alcoholism is a chronic, relapsing
condition with many similarities to asthma, diabetes and
high blood pressure.

Stigma also has led to inequities in the way the American
health care system addresses alcoholism. Unlike people with
other chronic illnesses, people with alcoholism who do seek
medical treatment face insurance restrictions at both the
public and private level.

Because alcoholism has not been addressed as a health issue, 75% of people with serious drinking problems never receive any treatment.

Alcoholism Is Similar to Asthma, Diabetes, and High Blood Pressure

Simply defined, a chronic disease is one that continues over
a long time, progresses consistently or intermittently, and
often can be managed. The causes of chronic disease can be
complex and include hereditary factors. A patient may not
experience many symptoms until the disease has advanced. A
chronic disease doesn't always follow a predictable course.
Some patients may relapse more frequently than others.
Treatment may require that patients change their behavior.

In each of these respects, alcoholism strongly resembles
such chronic diseases as asthma, diabetes and high blood
pressure among adults.

Although a single gene or set of genes has not been found that causes alcoholism, the risk for developing alcoholism is estimated to be 50 to 60 percent genetic. The genetic risks for developing asthma, diabetes and high blood pressure are comparable. As with many other complex illnesses in which family history is a factor, there appear to be a number of genetically controlled characteristics that make some individuals more vulnerable to becoming dependent on alcohol.

People who know they are at genetic risk for asthma, diabetes and high blood pressure can control certain risk factors. Similarly, individuals with family histories of alcoholism can reduce their risk by choosing not to drink or strictly limiting the amount that they drink. This may be easier said than done, however, particularly for young people, who may lack the maturity to make responsible decisions about their health. People use alcohol to feel good, at least initially, and many believe American society encourages drinking.

Alcohol is an addictive drug. Over time, its use can lead to craving and impaired control. Even if the decision to drink is voluntary at first, what happens after someone takes a drink depends to a large extent on an individual's genetic vulnerability to alcoholism, and how one's body and mind react to alcohol. . . .

The Treatment Plan Must Be Carefully Followed

Like people with other chronic diseases, individuals with alcoholism who follow treatment recommendations, including education, counseling and medication, show significant improvement during treatment and for 6–12 months afterwards. Forty to 60 percent remain continuously abstinent after a year; another 15–30 percent resume drinking (though not at levels at which they become dependent again). Patients who do return to drinking usually haven't complied with the behavior changes or medications that have been prescribed to them.

Whether or not persons with asthma, high blood pressure or diabetes improve also depends on how well they follow their doctors' orders. In an article published by the *Journal of the American Medical Association* comparing addiction to these conditions, the authors noted that fewer than 40 percent of patients with asthma or high blood pressure take their medications as prescribed. Diabetics do a little better: nearly 60 percent take their insulin, perhaps because they quickly feel worse physically if they don't. But no group follows recommendations to change their behavior and/or diet very well. Fewer than 30 percent of adults with asthma, diabetes or high blood pressure are able to make the behavioral changes necessary to improve their health and prevent the re-occurrence of symptoms.

Alcoholism Was Called a Disease in 1784

Although first use of the term "alcoholism" is attributed to a nineteenth century Swedish physician, ancient Romans recognized the difference between people who drank too much by choice and people who couldn't control their drinking. Centuries later, the Middle English language distinguished between drunkenness and addiction to drink. And as early as 1784, Dr. Benjamin Rush, the father of American psychiatry and a signer of the Declaration of Independence, described habitual drinking as an involuntary condition, a disease caused by "spirituous liquors."

National Council on Alcoholism and Drug Dependence, Inc., 2000.

Patient difficulty in following doctors' orders may explain why relapse rates for these conditions are similar to those for alcoholism. During the course of a year, 30–50 percent of adults with diabetes and 50–70 percent of adults with high blood pressure or asthma will suffer a re-occurrence of their symptoms severe enough to require medical intervention, sometimes including hospitalization.

Despite the numerous points of similarity between alcoholism and other chronic diseases, it is important to remember some significant differences. Although early changes in behavior patterns can prevent or ameliorate these diseases, once adults with asthma, diabetes or high blood pressure advance to a certain stage, behavior change alone is not sufficient to treat them. Medication must be prescribed for their health to improve.

Some people with alcoholism, however, stop drinking without formal medical treatment. Lack of formal medical treatment and limited health insurance coverage has meant that Alcoholics Anonymous and other support groups often have been the only help available to people with alcoholism. But it would be shortsighted and tragic to interpret some people's success with support groups alone as evidence to maintain the status quo.

Sound public health policy for chronic illnesses is not based on self-help behavior change alone. If it were, rates of uncontrolled high blood pressure, diabetes and asthma would soar.

Alcoholism Should Be Treated as a Chronic Disease

Early intervention is essential in preventing alcohol problems, including alcoholism, just as it is for other chronic diseases. But while a blood pressure test to diagnose hypertension is part of routine medical practice, fewer than 30 percent of primary care physicians carefully screen their patients for health problems related to their use of alcohol or other drugs.

A number of effective screening instruments, including written questionnaires that can be administered and evaluated in less than five minutes during a regular office visit, are readily available. These screening instruments can help primary care physicians identify problem drinking in its early stages, when brief interventions can help patients cut back on their drinking before they become physically dependent on alcohol.

Screening instruments also are crucial in helping primary care physicians form a preliminary diagnosis of alcoholism. If screening indicates that a patient has alcoholism, a more extensive diagnostic assessment using criteria developed by the American Psychiatric Association will be necessary. Patients who appear to be alcoholic should be referred to an addiction specialist for this purpose and encouraged to attend Alcoholics Anonymous and other support groups. . . .

Lack of widespread screening and brief interventions, however, has meant that alcoholism is treated more often as an acute illness than a chronic disease. Medical intervention frequently occurs only when an individual becomes seriously ill, and detoxification is necessary. Detoxification, which typically lasts three to five days, helps patients overcome their physiological and psychological dependence on alcohol. Generally, detoxification takes place under medical supervision. Brief hospitalization may be required for some severely addicted individuals; for others, treatment can be completed on an outpatient basis.

Following detoxification, patients often are left to their own devices. Some find their way to specialty treatment or Alcoholics Anonymous or other support groups and stay sober for as long as they remain in rehabilitation. But upon discharge, much as if they just had a cast removed from a broken arm, their treatment comes to an end. Six to 12 months later, their recovery is evaluated by a single criterion: have they been continuously abstinent?

A Relapse Does Not Mean That Treatment Has Failed

Failure to understand alcoholism as a chronic disease has contributed to a perception that treatment is ineffective, and that people don't quit drinking because they are weak-willed and don't try hard enough. If a person resumes drinking after detoxification, many would judge such a relapse to be evidence that treatment has failed. The opposite holds true for adults with asthma, diabetes and high pressure: relapse indicates that further treatment is necessary. Effective health care practitioners don't expect such patients to remain in good health without continued medical monitoring and periodic intervention.

The force of stigma cannot be underestimated in any discussion of alcoholism. Intoxication, as well as the destructive effects of alcohol, increase the visibility of alcoholism. On the other hand, patients who achieve abstinence or reduce their drinking typically disappear from view. Support groups actively encourage anonymity. Such anonymity makes it almost impossible to collect reliable scientific data and difficult to build constituency groups to form and improve public policies for alcohol problems and treatment. In the public eye, individuals who successfully control their chronic illness of alcoholism are rarely visible, while those who still struggle and have relapses are easy to see and to remember.

One of the most insidious ways that stigma becomes apparent is through the discriminatory way health insurance covers alcoholism. For example, Medicare pays just 50 percent of outpatient treatment costs for alcoholism but 80 percent for other medical conditions. Individuals with private health insurance confront benefit limitations on alcohol treatment that do not exist for other chronic diseases even though full equality in coverage (parity) could be achieved for an overall cost increase of 0.3 percent in health insurance premiums.

The limits and barriers in employment-based health insurance and in public health insurance programs such as Medicare mean that, once people are motivated to seek treatment, they may not be able to get the help they need. Without treatment and continued medical monitoring, the chance of relapse increases significantly.

As the nation seeks to improve treatment for diabetes, hypertension, asthma, and other chronic illnesses, it is time to include alcoholism among that group of chronic treatable illnesses.

"A model based on integrating psychological, biological, and social factors for understanding and treating chemical dependency, addictions, and compulsive behaviors is more appropriate than a disease model."

Alcoholism Should Not Be Treated as a Disease

Edward A. Dreyfus

Alcoholism was originally labeled a disease in order to convince alcohol abusers that they had a serious problem and should seek help, Edward A. Dreyfus asserts in the following viewpoint. However, he maintains, now the disease metaphor is being overused and wrongly applied to such behaviors as overeating, smoking, and drinking. Further, he argues that increasing numbers of alcoholics and others with compulsive disorders and substance abuse problems are beginning to think that they are sick and are seeking medical rather than the psychological help they need. Edward A. Dreyfus is a clinical psychologist in private practice in California.

As you read, consider the following questions:
1. In the author's opinion what does the disease model fail to take into account about compulsive behavior?
2. Why is the disease model inappropriate for compulsive behaviors, in Dreyfus's opinion?
3. According to the author, what must people be ready to do if they choose to live life differently than most without being labeled "sick"?

Edward A. Dreyfus, "Keeping Your Sanity: Essays for Better Living," www.docdreyfus.com, 2000. Copyright © 2000 by Edward A. Dreyfus. Reproduced by permission.

M any mental health practitioners are promoting the notion that alcohol abuse, drug abuse, over-eating, gambling, anorexia, bulimia and smoking are diseases. By using the disease model, its proponents believe that people are more apt to seek help because having an "illness" is more acceptable than having psychological or behavior disorder. I am reminded of the effects of saying that people with emotional difficulties were "sick," and suffering from a "disease." Psychology and psychiatry moved a long way forward when we listened to Thomas Szasz declare that mental illness was a myth, to Karl Menninger discussing degrees of personality organization, and to Benjamin Rush when he spoke of problems in living. Now it appears we are moving backwards. What will be the next "disease" to appear in the news media?

The disease model states that alcoholism and compulsive over-eating, for example, are diseases and can be compared to diabetes in that diabetics react to sugar in a similar way that over-eaters have a reaction to food and alcoholics to liquor. Therefore, in both instances the individuals must carefully monitor their intake. If they do not rigidly adhere to their respective diets there will be dire consequences. The compulsive over-eater, for example, maintains that if he/she does not monitor food intake, there is a chemical imbalance which takes over and control over one's eating is no longer possible. So, the theory maintains, the compulsive over-eater is not "normal" insofar as eating is concerned, but rather he or she has a "disease" and is "sick."

The question that this thesis does not address, however, is: Why do compulsive over-eaters and alcoholics, knowing that they are not able to control their substance abuse once it is started, persist in breaking their diet? The diabetic's disease is the failure of the body to produce sufficient insulin; the disease is not the individual's failure to stay on a diabetic diet. It is not the *behavior* that is the disease, it is the manner in which the body metabolizes alcohol that may be the disease, leading to the necessity for dietary control, or in the case of the substance abuser and alcoholic, abstinence. While there may be a biological or chemical basis for some compulsions, the disease model does not account for the compulsive *behavior* itself; it only accounts for the specific substance.

Historical Perspective

Many years ago mentally disturbed persons were considered to be inhabited by the devil; they were ostracized from their communities and families and were treated with disdain. They were locked up, deprived of their human rights, and often killed. Pinel [a French physician], in the 18th century, cut the chains of the inmates of the insane asylum at Bicitre and freed them, declaring that they were not possessed of evil spirits, but rather that they were medically ill. This was the beginning of a movement which sought to achieve humane treatment for the mentally disturbed. It was an extremely important step forward. By declaring these people ill, the indignities they suffered were reduced. It was *necessary* to call them "sick" in order to obtain humane treatment.

As the theories of Sigmund Freud were made available and became acceptable, it was discovered that many of these individuals were not ill in the medical sense, but rather they were psychologically disturbed. The "talking cure," as psychoanalysis was then called, demonstrated that mental "illness" could be cured through words. This was another very important step, for now, people with psychological disorders could be viewed with some dignity and could potentially be treated by nonmedical practitioners. Unfortunately neither the patients nor the practitioners were accorded the same respect as those with physical ailments who were being treated by physicians. In fact, many people still believe it is much more acceptable to be physically ill than it is to be psychologically disturbed.

So, instead of being chained in dungeons and forgotten, the mentally ill were locked in hospitals and treated. However, it gradually became obvious that they were still ostracized from the community, and were being treated as second class citizens. Though they were treated better physically, they still carried the stigma of being "sick," which was almost as dehumanizing as being thought of as "inhabited by the devil." Now they were pitied, but they still lost their freedom, their dignity, and their human rights.

The movement away from the disease model toward a psychological model helped pave the way toward integrating the "mentally ill" into the community rather than segregating them. It had the effect of gaining more respect, understanding, and dignity for all people with emotional difficulties. Instead of seeing these people as "sick," we began seeing them as having "problems in living," which could be understood and resolved. Such a psychological model permitted greater numbers of nonmedical practitioners to "treat" these individuals and has made such treatment more available and more affordable to more people. People began to feel more comfortable treating troubled people humanly without having to see them as "sick." (In fact, they found that the disease model interfered with effective treatment.) People trying to cope with internal or external stress may do so in maladaptive ways. This does not make them "sick."

Consequences of a Disease Model

When it came to compulsive behaviors, however, even the most compassionate individuals had difficulty accepting that people did not seem able to control their own behavior. Hence, they treated alcoholics as "bums," over-eaters as "fatsos," gamblers as "stupid," etc. And these people viewed themselves similarly. So, the concept of illness was invoked once again. And once again people were treated for their "illness" and others viewed them more compassionately as, "Don't laugh at your overweight Aunt Mary, she has an illness," or "Your drunk Uncle Charley is sick." I think it is pitiful that a society has to resort to seeing people as sick in order to be compassionate towards them. And I believe it adversely affects people's self-esteem to have to consider themselves sick in order to be related to humanly. I find it sad that people, so hungry for acceptance, both self-acceptance or acceptance from others, will accept the appellation "sick."

The advocates for various self-help and other groups that deal with compulsive substance abuse view these compulsions as diseases. They promote the concept of disease in order to entice substance abusers into treatment. If they can convince these people that they are "sick" and they are suffering from a "disease" then it is believed that more people will accept treatment.

We live in a society that loves labels whether on clothes or on people. We tend to relate to the clothes people, with the labels on the outside, just as we treat the labels we pin on people: schizophrenic, alcoholic, ACA [adult child of an alcoholic], incest survivor, borderline personality, etc. And people seem to need to view themselves as "sick" in order to be treated humanly (and in order to treat themselves with care.)

Psychology strove for years to move away from the medical/disease model so that healers would relate to people as people, not as labels, not as "sick." This was called the humanistic movement and eschewed the medical model and sought a psychological model. I see a reversal of this effort and find it regressive. And I think, in this context, that 12-step programs with their emphasis on disease and "sickness," fosters this regressive type of thinking.

While I do not object to the results or even some of the methods employed, I do object to the use of the terms "disease" and "sick" as a means for effecting these results. There are consequences to using a disease model which extend beyond merely controlling substance abuse. In our quest for expediency, we are often short-sighted.

Social Consequences

I object to the idea that compulsive *behavior* is a disease. It does not matter whether there is a chemical imbalance that leaves these people vulnerable to gaining weight and drinking, the disease concept is not appropriate for the compulsive behaviors. Society decides on what is compulsive, and using the disease concept, any one of us could be viewed as "sick" for any behavior that people deem compulsive. Thus someone who is a "workaholic," a smoker, or a nail-biter could be considered "sick." Don't people have the right to engage in activities, even unhealthy activities, without being considered "sick"?

Compulsive behavior is rewarded in our society. Indeed, people are taught to be compulsive; that is, we are taught to be punctual, orderly, committed, organized, etc. We are taught to hide our feelings through activity. We are taught to keep busy when we are feeling badly. We are taught to whistle when afraid, think about something else when we are sad, and even to eat when we are "blue." All compulsive individuals are taught at an early age to deny feelings through some form of activity. And if you learn your lessons well, you could be considered "sick."

Psychological Consequences

Some psychological consequences of the disease model are:

1. Individuals tend to give up responsibility for their life; they can see themselves as victims because the "disease" is not their fault.

2. Individuals seek someone to "fix" them without examining the causes or issues which may produce the compulsion; only the symptom is examined.

3. There is a loss of dignity and self-esteem in believing that one is "bad" or "sick" for having gone off a diet, or drinking, etc.

4. Individuals often use "illness" or "disease" to avoid taking responsibility for their behavior just as they might have gotten "sick" to avoid going to school.

5. This kind of infantilization has long-term consequences to one's self-esteem and self-confidence, though it may have immediate results. Patronizing others does not enhance one's self-concept.

6. By seeing oneself as "sick," one invites compassion and pity; and one then begins to see oneself as pitiful, hoping for a magical cure that someday will be discovered if one is "good."

Because we live in a society that also looks askew at individuals with psychological problems, especially compulsive disorders (they tend to be viewed as lacking in will-power or lacking in moral fiber), it is much more palatable to talk in terms of the "disease" which needs to be treated than it is to deal with maladaptive coping behaviors. It is more acceptable to go to the medical doctor's office than it is to go to the psychotherapist's office. So the disease model has much more appeal for the majority of our society.

Thus, what started out as a humane approach to a problem has become in itself a problem. Originally, calling compulsive behaviors a disease was for the purpose of increasing compassion toward the obese, the alcoholic, or the gambler. Gradually the solution has produced the very effect it sought to eliminate—namely, reducing human dignity and reinforcing the notion that one is not a responsible adult. Rather, the compulsive substance abuser is viewed as a helpless child who is "sick" and needs to be told what to do. (In fact, in some of these self-help programs, members are referred to as "babies.")

Alcoholism Is a Behavior, Not a Disease

Alcoholism is a behavior. Behaviors are not disease entities, they are bad habits perseverated by obsessive repetition and habituation. Habituated, substance induced behaviors cannot be reduced to a single etiology anymore than non-substance induced behaviors can be reduced to a single etiology. Sex, eating, gambling, computers, computer games, and unrequited love are normative behaviors that have been declared diseases. Sex, gambling, computers, computer games, and unrequited love do not involve the ingestion of any substance yet abstinence from these habituated behaviors may incite withdrawal symptoms identical to substance withdrawal symptoms. The answer to the eradication of alcoholism lies in our national perspective of alcoholism. Do we want to perpetuate the myth of alcoholism being a disease entity that is out of the realm of one's discretional, volitional control or do we tell the truth? Do we let the dirty secret out of the bag and tell everyone that, like Dorothy in the Wizard of Oz, they already possess the power to hold dominion over alcoholism?

Holden Massachusetts Police Department, April 7, 2003. www.holdenpd.com.

There is no doubt that were we to promote a psychological model of abuse rather than a disease model, many individuals would not seek treatment; that would be their choice. However, in my opinion, there is greater harm to many more people from the potential loss of responsibility, choice, and dignity by invoking a disease model. What will be the next "sickness" for which treatment will be given? When do we have the right to behave differently than society dictates without being labeled "sick"?

Political Consequences

If we accept a "disease" model for compulsive behavior, then what will stop people from thinking about other psychological disorders as disease? And if this happens, we will be back where we were 50 years ago, believing that all people with emotional problems are "sick." Who will treat these "sick" people? Clearly the medical profession has a vested interest in promoting a disease model, for it is physicians who treat the "sick." It does not matter to the public that the "disease model" was only a *metaphor* used to encourage people to seek help. Over time the metaphor is lost and we are left with a model that is inappropriate. While the idea of using a disease model as a metaphor, to make it more palatable for some people to accept treatment, has some short range appeal, the long range consequences may be less attractive.

Many people do not comprehend the use of the disease model as a metaphor or as a theoretical model for generating hypotheses. Metaphors and models often become functionally autonomous; they take on a reality of their own. Yesterday's metaphors become today's reality. As the use of the term "disease" increases, and with more public acceptance of the notion that compulsive behaviors are diseases, we must become concerned with the long term consequences on our thinking about the relationship between emotional disorders and disease.

Are we heading toward a time when, once again, people with problems in living and emotionally disturbed human beings will be viewed as "sick" and in need of medical, not psychological, treatment?

An Alternative Model

I think that a model based on integrating psychological, biological, and social factors for understanding and treating chemical dependency, addictions, and compulsive behaviors is more appropriate than a disease model. Such a model takes into account biological (including genetics, physiological predisposition, and chemical components), social, and psychological factors in understanding compulsive behaviors without invoking "sickness" or disease as causative. The individual, in this model, remains responsible for how he/she deals with their life without the loss in dignity.

This model accepts that there may be genetic, chemical, biological, etc. factors involved in some addictions (for not being able to metabolize alcohol, for example), but this does not account for why an individual continues to rely upon their addiction for dealing with problems in living. It recognizes that there are social issues involved in compulsive behavior which have nothing to do with biology or chemistry. It further states that psychological, not medical, factors are the most powerful in understanding and controlling human behavior. It accepts the basic principle that human beings are fundamentally responsible for their own behavior and have the power to choose how they will conduct their lives. It accepts that people are free to choose how they will live their life; even if that choice is self-destructive, it is still their choice. People can choose to play the game of life differently than most without being labeled "sick." They must, however, accept full responsibility for the consequences of that behavior.

> *"AA succeeds where most other programs fail because the reach for sobriety is only the beginning."*

Alcoholics Anonymous Is Effective

Robby Werner

Alcoholics Anonymous (AA) is effective because it provides the emotional and spiritual support and fellowship many alcoholics need to achieve sobriety, Robby Werner argues in the following viewpoint. Werner contends that the program's Twelve Steps provide alcoholics with a way to reinvent their personalities and rebuild their lives. He maintains that alcoholics learn how to live without alcohol by helping each other work the Twelve Steps. Robby Werner is a journalist and occasional contributor to the *Journal Inquirer* in Manchester, Connecticut.

As you read, consider the following questions:
1. According to the author, what feeling do alcoholics express most often as they tell their stories?
2. What is a blackout, according to Werner?
3. How long does recovery from alcoholism take, according to the author?

They are male and female, doctors and dockhands, punk rockers and patricians, young and old. They are drill sergeants and captains of industry sharing generalities and private demons. They are black and white and Spanish-speaking. Some of them went to Yale and others have been to jail. They face each dawn stepping forward on a journey whose only destination is day's end and the uncertain promise of beginning tomorrow as they began today. They undertake the effort as if their very survival depends on it. It does.

They introduce themselves as Jack T. or Molly R. and bring new meaning to "first-name basis." In Connecticut alone, they gather in groups some 2000 times a week to find in each other human way stations to re-fuel their resolve. They are people you know. They are Alcoholics Anonymous.

A few weeks ago I asked an old friend I knew was very involved in AA to take me to a meeting. I had hoped to pick up a column's worth of anecdotes and maybe a few details about some drunks who were trying to stay sober. I looked around the room at that first meeting and saw tattooed bikers, yuppies, senior citizens and teenagers scattered evenly among the dozen or so tables set up in a church basement. I soon realized an issue that could produce fellowship in a group like this was going to be more complex than expected. I collected a pile of literature, borrowed several tapes of AA speakers and attended several more meetings all over Connecticut.

Some alcoholics will attempt to get sober and fail; others will never try. Most will die drunk. A few million of them—a small percentage of the total—will find recovery in the AA program.

Alcoholics are not just people who drink a lot. Liquor does not produce in them a mellow buzz or a bold euphoria. It goes down their throat and resounds with the "Pow! Zing!" of a genie being released from a bottle. And this personal Aladdin's Lamp, this elixir, simply takes over. "Go ahead Eve," it whispers, "take another bite out of that apple."

Imagine the temptation of ready access to a potion which could instantly imprison your problems in a liquid suspension. Even if you knew it would kill you, and those very problems would soon boomerang bigger and meaner from neglect. How many of us could say no to such a temporary remedy, however lethal in some far-flung future it might be? Who could deny themselves a cure for financial troubles, a contentious marriage or feelings of self-doubt? If this sounds easy ask yourself why there are cigarette smokers and remember tobacco's effects are not anywhere near as satisfying as alcohol to the drinker.

Alcoholics Often Feel Lonely

As one listens to alcoholics tell their stories an oft-recurring theme is a feeling of aloneness, of being different, singled out, picked on or not being good enough. They see themselves as losers in the unwinnable endgame of, in the words of Clancy I., "comparing the way you feel on the inside to the way other people appear on the outside." When they have a few and often, a few more, these feelings go away. It is the recipe for an alcoholic.

The alcoholic, like an athlete who overuses painkillers, drinks to stay in the game.

The halfback knows he risks being unable to walk again and the alcoholic may be aware he props himself up on clay feet, but the fangs of his inner serpent lace him with a venom for which the only antidote is drink.

The alcoholic will tell himself he's not like the others who have "that" weakness. He will be convinced he can stop at any time; that he only hits the sauce because he has all these damnable problems. He's sure he is different. If he ever hits rock-bottom and begins on the Alcoholics Anonymous path to sobriety he will learn his mindset is the essential definition of alcoholism.

He is like them: It is not the High Life or the highball at the root of his condition. He is irresistibly attracted to alcohol.

There are as many ways to hit bottom as there are alcoholics. It might be a series of car wrecks or one in which an innocent is killed or injured. It can be absenteeism and the loss of employment. Maybe it's an instance of domestic abuse so heinous the perpetrator feels as if it was someone else who committed it. The household budget perhaps was spent at a bar instead of for housing or baby food.

Possibly there was such a craving for drink the individual found himself quaffing after-shave or mouthwash. It might mean an unsettling wake-up from a blackout.

A blackout is an episode in which the actor is so out of it he has no self-awareness and later will have no memory of his actions. She may even appear to the casual observer to be functioning normally. It is not unheard of for an alcoholic to come to from a blackout aboard an airplane bound for an unknown destination, behind the wheel of a car with steam spurting from a radiator which has just been introduced at high speed to the side of a ditch or in the bed of a stranger surrounded by four unfamiliar walls.

The alcoholic who finds himself in this gutter need only to raise one finger above the curb to seek help. If he can reach within himself to reach that far, he will find the ready hand of Alcoholics Anonymous. Here, he can meet the many others who are like him and in their fellowship set out on a new road to sobriety. This route is called The Twelve Steps.

The Steps are not rungs on a ladder to be climbed to a fixed destination. They are dance steps practiced again and again every day of the recovering alcoholic's life.

AA succeeds where most other programs fail because the reach for sobriety is only the beginning. Anyone can turn out dry people—hospitals, treatment facilities and lock-ups do it all the time. But in a matter of hours or days after release, they will have fallen off the wagon.

The Twelve Steps Help the Alcoholic Reinvent His Personality

The Steps can be enumerated and related but not truly described by an outsider any more than one can explain the instant in which one learns to ride a bicycle.

Recovering alcoholics spend years practicing step sobriety and attend certain meetings dedicated to helping one another learn the process. The Steps are not so much about stopping drinking—"alcohol" is mentioned but once in the text—as they are a daily methodology to reinvent the alcoholic personality. Recovery is a lifelong seminar.

Just as an adolescent learns how to drink, the alcoholic learns how not to: One day at a time.

Step One: *We admitted we were powerless over alcohol—that our lives had become unmanageable.* Since the Twelve Steps' ultimate goal is to rebuild a personality, the recovering alcoholic must first admit she has hit bottom. This serves as a foundation upon which to build a new and sober individual. A building rehabilitated from halfway up on shaky underpinnings will surely crumble.

Step Two: *Came to believe that a Power greater than ourselves could restore us to sanity.* The newcomer must begin to believe there is something out there to help him recover from his addiction. For many, this means God. For some, it is Alcoholics Anonymous and the support of his fellow sufferers. This step opens the door of faith and the realization that recovery is possible.

Length of Sobriety of Alcoholics Anonymous Members in 2001

48% Sober more than 5 years

22% Sober between 1–5 years

30% Sober less than 1 year

Average sobriety of members is more than *seven* years.

Based on a random survey of 7,500 Alcoholics Anonymous members in the United States and Canada.

Alcoholics Anonymous World Services, Inc., 2003.

Step Three: *Made a decision to turn our will and our lives over to the care of God as we understood him.* AA members often speak of their "Higher Power." Usually, this means God in the traditional sense but the underlined phrase of Step Three acknowledges God can be embraced in myriad ways. Some see God residing within all living things or as a tenant of the individual soul. Many atheists and agnostics are also successful members of AA Step Three, for the alcoholic, is the first part of a quest to discover a weapon powerful enough to vanquish the demons which have brought his life to ruin.

Step Four: *Made a fearless and searching moral inventory of ourselves.* Some failing deep inside the psyche of the alcoholic makes liquor a siren's song luring her to an eventual death. What lurks within her that she tries to suppress or escape with alcohol? At Step Four she tries to find out.

Step Five: *Admitted to God, to ourselves, and to another human being the exact nature of our wrongs.* Sometimes the best way for someone to understand what he does is to explain it to someone else. One of the steepest barriers to an alcoholic's recovery is often an unshakable feeling of being alone—even when surrounded by others. Step Five is a sledgehammer placed in the hands of the alcoholic to be wielded against the walls of isolation.

Step Six: *Were entirely ready to have God remove all these defects of character.* This does not suggest obtaining perfection or removing all flaws of the human condition. Rather, it opens in the alcoholic a willingness to try. If the life of the alcoholic is to be turned around it will happen slowly and deliberately, like a turret on a battleship.

Step Seven: *Humbly asked Him to remove our shortcomings.* The emphasis of Step Seven is humility. The alcoholic possessed of hubris will run the risk of tending to his own needs and probably return to his life in a bottle.

Step Eight: *Made a list of all persons we had harmed, and became willing to make amends to them all.*

Asking Forgiveness Is Difficult

Step Nine: *Made direct amends to such people wherever possible, except when to do so would injure them or others.* For most people the wronging of others, if they are even aware of it, is merely a cause of guilt or some other bad feeling. For the alcoholic who has come to know himself and his past, the harm he has done to others is a wild weed that threatens the garden of his new consciousness. Many members of AA feel Steps Eight and Nine are the most salutary and they are usually pleased and surprised by the positive support given them by those to whom they make amends. The exception to Step Nine is a judgment call: A clear case for its application would be not to apologize for having an affair with your best friend's wife if it still remains a secret.

Step Ten: *Continued to take personal inventory and when we were wrong promptly admitted it.* Recovery from alcoholism takes a lifetime. AA members must recognize their lives are now akin to a gymnast on the balance beam and one misstep could easily send them atumble into the waiting arms of John Barleycorn. Step Ten is a daily or even hourly exercise in which the alcoholic takes note of where she's been, where she is and where she must go.

Step Eleven: *Sought through prayer and meditation to improve our conscious contact with God as we understood him, praying only for knowledge of His will for us and the power to carry that out.* All members of AA focus on different steps to varying degrees. Some interpret this step to mean elevating their level of prayer as it is defined in the traditional sense and strengthening the communication between themselves and their God. Others look inward in their meditations.

Step Twelve: *Having had a spiritual awakening as the result of these steps, we tried to carry this message to alcoholics, and to practice these principles in all our affairs.* The recovering alcoholic learns giving is its own reward. Service to others is an integral part of his sobriety. Some of this is accomplished through the sponsorship practice of AA in which a new member asks a veteran to be his guide and mentor. The sponsor makes himself available to his sponsee twenty-four hours a day, seven days a week and provides succor and sanctuary for his charge in times of temptation. In doing so, the sponsor fortifies his own sobriety through the discipline of promising to be there for someone else. Just as a new parent moves further into maturity, the sponsor learns the discipline of dependability.

This article . . . is a mere distillation of an enormously complex and ill-understood condition and its treatment. Alcoholics Anonymous is not without its failures . . . and its critics. It is however, the only "cure" for alcoholics with any consistent record for success.

"The best evidence available suggests that AA is ineffective as a means of overcoming alcohol problems, and there's some evidence that exposure to AA worsens . . . binge drinking."

Alcoholics Anonymous Is Ineffective

Charles Bufe

Alcoholics Anonymous (AA) is not only ineffective in helping people overcome alcohol problems, in some instances it actually makes their problems worse, Charles Bufe argues in the following viewpoint. He contends that the success rate for alcoholics in AA is no better—and could actually be worse—than that of alcoholics who get no treatment at all. Further, AA members are much more likely to revert to binge drinking than are alcoholics seeking other forms of treatment. Charles Bufe is the founder of See Sharp Press and the author of *Alcoholics Anonymous: Cult or Cure*, from which this viewpoint is excerpted.

As you read, consider the following questions:

1. What does the author argue is a noticeable feature of AA regarding membership?
2. How does AA define success in overcoming an alcohol problem, in Charles Bufe's opinion?
3. What does Charles Bufe argue is one reason that there have been few scientific investigations of AA effectiveness?

Estimates of AA's Effectiveness

It does seem possible to draw at least tentative conclusions about the effectiveness of Alcoholics Anonymous. A good starting point is AA's most recently announced membership figures. As of January 1, 1996, AA claimed 1.251 million members in the U.S. and Canada while there were approximately 218 million individuals 18 years of age and over in the two countries at that time. Taking the ARF [Addiction Research Foundation] estimates of the percentages of alcohol abusers and alcohol-dependent persons and multiplying them by total population figures yields a total of roughly 22 million individuals with alcohol problems in 1996; doing the same calculations using the NIAAA [National Institute on Alcohol Abuse and Alcoholism] percentages yields a total of roughly 16.13 million persons. Taking these as high and low estimates of the number of alcohol abusers, as of the date of the last available AA membership figures, somewhere between 5.7% and 7.7% of U.S. and Canadian "alcoholics" belonged to AA. And the percentage of those who will reach the AA goal of lifelong abstinence is much lower than that.

A noticeable feature of AA is that a large number of its members have been in the organization for a relatively short time. Based on my attendance at AA meetings in San Francisco in the late 1980s, I would estimate that over 50% of those attending meetings in that city at that time were members for less than one year and, in fact, that a majority were members for only a few months. The situation appears to have changed little in recent years. (The discrepancy between my observations and AA's claim that only 27% of its members have less than one-year's abstinence is probably accounted for by AA's astoundingly high dropout rate; because of it, one constantly sees new faces showing up at AA meetings, with many of them sticking around for relatively few meetings.)

My estimate, however, isn't too far out of line with the figures given by Bill C.[1] in a 1965 article in the *Quarterly Journal of Studies on Alcohol*. In it, he reports that of 393 AA members surveyed, 31% had been sober for more than one year; 12% had been sober for more than one year but had

---

1. AA members use only first names and last initials to protect their anonymity.

had at least one relapse after joining AA; 9% had achieved a year's sobriety; 6% had died; 3% had gone to prison; 1% had gone to mental institutions; and 38% had stopped attending AA. What makes these numbers even more dismal than they appear is the fact that Bill C. defined a member as someone who attended 10 or more AA meetings in a year's time. When you take into account the "revolving door effect," it becomes apparent that far more persons attended AA meetings than the 393 "members" Bill C. lists. It seems quite probable that he picked the figure of 10 meetings in a year as a membership criterion because AA's success rate would have been revealed as microscopic if he had used a smaller number of attendances as his membership-defining device. (It should also be mentioned that attendance at 10 meetings in itself seems to imply a fairly high degree of motivation.)

Most Alcoholics Have Tried AA

The success rate calculated through analysis of the 1996 AA membership survey is hardly more impressive. The survey brochure indicates that 45% of members have at least five years' sobriety. Using the figure of five years' sobriety as the criterion of success, one arrives at an AA success rate of approximately 2.6% to 3.5% (in comparison with the total number of "alcoholics" in the U.S. and Canada). And the success rate is lower than that if one defines "success" as AA does—as lifelong abstinence.

It could be argued that this is an unfair way of evaluating the effectiveness of AA, and that only "alcoholics" who have investigated AA should be considered. That's a reasonable argument, but there's evidence that a very high proportion of "alcoholics" *have* at one time or another checked into AA. Anyone who has attended many AA meetings can testify that droves of newcomers show up, attend one, or a few, meeting(s), and then are never seen again—the "revolving door effect." As well, roughly 270,000 individuals accused or convicted of drunk driving and other alcohol-related crimes are coerced into 12-step treatment every year in the United States. Based on the sheer numbers of such persons, it seems probable that well over 50%, perhaps as many as 90%, of American and Canadian problem drinkers investigate AA at some time during their drinking careers.

There's statistical evidence to indicate that this is so. Well known researcher Robin Room, of the Addiction Research Foundation, reports that a 1990 survey of 2058 Americans aged 18 and over revealed that 9% of American adults have attended an AA meeting at some time in their lives, and that an astounding 3.4% claimed to have done so in the previous year. (The latter percentage is almost certainly incorrect.) If Room's 9% figure is even close to being correct, it's good evidence that a very high percentage of U.S. and Canadian alcohol abusers have attended AA at least once. In 1996, 9% of American and Canadian adults corresponded to roughly 19.6 million individuals. This figure, when compared with the previously mentioned estimates of alcohol abusers and alcohol-dependent persons (16.13 to 22 million individuals), provides persuasive evidence that the percentage of "alcoholics" who have tried AA is high indeed—and that AA's success rate is very low.

AA's Triennial Surveys Show Little Success

AA's own statistics provide perhaps the most persuasive evidence that AA's success rate is minuscule. Since 1977, AA has conducted an extensive survey of its members every three years (though the survey scheduled for 1995 was conducted in 1996). These surveys measure such things as length of membership, age distribution, male-female ratio, employment categories, and length of sobriety. Following the 1989 survey, AA produced a large monograph, "Comments on A.A.'s Triennial Surveys," that analyzed the results of all five surveys done to that point. In terms of new-member dropout rate, all five surveys were in close agreement. According to the "Comments" document, the "% of those coming to AA within the first year that have remained the indicated number of months" is 19% after one month; 10% after three months; and 5% after 12 months. In other words, AA has a 95% new-member dropout rate during the first year of attendance.

If success is defined as one-year's sobriety, on the face of it this 95% dropout rate gives AA a *maximum* success rate of only 5%; and a great many new members do not remain continuously sober during their first year in AA, which causes the apparent AA success rate to fall even lower. Of course, many of the 95% who drop out within the first year are probably "repeaters" who have previously investigated AA, and this would increase the apparent AA success rate; but at least for the present there is no way to know what percentage of the dropouts are repeaters. Additionally, at least some of the 95% who drop out of AA during their first year do manage to sober up; but to date there's no way to know what their numbers are. As well, it seems quite probable that most of those who drop out early in the program do so because they dislike and disagree with AA, so it could be argued that most of them who overcome their drinking problems do so in spite of, not because of, AA. Finally, at least some curiosity seekers and relatives of alcohol abusers show up at meetings, and this would further increase the apparent AA success rate. But to date, there are no reliable figures on what percentage of those who "walk through the door" fit those categories— though my personal estimate, and that of researcher/author Vince Fox, is that no more than 10% of new faces at AA meetings belong to relatives or curiosity seekers.

One thing, however, is certain: An extremely high percentage of American drinkers who have been hospitalized for alcoholism or who have participated in other institutional alcoholism programs have participated in Alcoholics Anonymous. The number of patients treated for alcoholism is now approximately 950,000 annually, which (because 12-step treatment is used in well over 90% of institutional programs) is a good indication that the proportion of alcohol abusers who have been exposed to AA is very high. It should also be kept in mind that in most parts of the country convicted drunk drivers are still routinely forced to attend AA as a condition of probation, which pushes the percentage of alcohol abusers exposed to AA even higher. Further, in most areas AA is the only widely available—and widely media-promoted—alcoholism self-help group, so AA has a very high volume of "walk in" traffic.

But let's give AA the benefit of the doubt and estimate that only 50% of U.S. and Canadian alcohol abusers have tried AA. That would double the success rate calculated earlier (based on the total number of U.S. and Canadian alcohol abusers), and it would increase to 5.2% to 7.0% if the criterion of success is defined as five years' sobriety.

In a worst case scenario, where 90% of U.S. and Canadian alcohol abusers have tried AA, where success is defined as five or more years of sobriety, where 45% of AA members have been sober for five or more years (as AA indicates), and where there are 22 million alcohol abusers in the two countries, the AA success rate would be about 2.9% (and even lower than that if the criterion of success is lifelong sobriety rather than five years' sobriety). The true success rate of AA is very probably somewhere between these two extremes, depending, of course, on how one defines "success"; that is, AA's success rate is probably somewhere between 2.9% and 7% (of those who have attended AA).

Spontaneous Remission Is Significant

This is far from impressive, especially when compared with the rate of "spontaneous remission." Contrary to popular belief "alcoholism" is *not* a progressive and incurable "disease." Many studies have been conducted on so-called spontaneous recovery by "alcoholics" (that is, recovery without treatment, which can refer to achievement of either abstinence or controlled drinking), and the consensus of these studies is that "spontaneous" recovery occurs in a significant percentage of alcohol abusers, though the calculated rates of recovery vary considerably. Other consistently supported conclusions are that the rate of alcohol abuse and alcohol dependence (or, to use the older term, "alcoholism") declines far faster than can be explained by mortality among individuals past the age of 40, and that "spontaneous" recovery normally occurs for identifiable reasons. In many cases, remission comes suddenly after a particularly dangerous or humiliating incident shocks the drinker into realization of the seriousness of his or her drinking problem. In other cases, recovery occurs as a result of religious conversion or as the result of an "existential" decision to quit based on a gradually increasing realization of the seriousness of the problem. One review of available literature estimates the rate of spontaneous recovery at 3.7% to 7.4% per *year.* More recently, a large-scale longitudinal study of over 4,000 adults with prior, significant, diagnosable alcohol dependence (the *National Longitudinal Alcoholism Epidemiological Survey*, conducted by the Census Bureau) reported that 20 years after the onset of alcohol dependence, 90% of those who never received treatment were either abstinent or "drinking without abuse or dependence." Compared with these figures, the above calculated rate of recovery via AA is not impressive. In fact, it appears to be no higher—and could actually be *lower*—than the rate of spontaneous remission.

Controlled Studies of AA's Effectiveness

But haven't there been scientific investigations of the effectiveness of AA? There have been, but there haven't been many. One reason for this could well be that "A.A. does not like to have researchers around," that it is highly reluctant to "open its doors to researchers." Whatever the truth of these charges, to date there have been only two well-designed studies of the effectiveness of AA—that is, studies which have included control groups and the random assignment of subjects. . . . Both controlled studies indicated that AA is *not* an effective across-the-board treatment for alcohol abuse or dependence ("alcoholism"). The subjects in both studies were, however, court-referred alcoholic offenders and hence different from the general alcoholic population in certain respects. Thus one distinguishing feature of the study populations is that they did not voluntarily seek treatment; they were forced to attend AA.

On the surface, these factors—the employment of coercion and the special-population status of alcoholic offenders—seem to lessen the credibility of the two controlled studies of AA's effectiveness. But it could be argued that one factor is irrelevant and the other actually enhances the studies' credibility. If, as is commonly asserted, AA is a universally applicable treatment for *all* alcoholics, the makeup of the study populations shouldn't have mattered a whit as long as the assignment of subjects to AA and control groups was truly random. And the fact that the studies' subjects were coerced into participating could well *increase* the validity of the studies' findings, because a very important biasing factor, subject motivation, was eliminated, and the remaining biasing factors were spread out fairly evenly among the groups studied because of the random assignment procedure. Further, since at least a third of present-day AA participants are coerced into attendance either by alcoholism treatment programs or the courts, through programs for DUI and other alcohol-related offenders, the populations of these studies were perhaps not as different from the general AA population as one might suspect.

Criticisms of Alcoholics Anonymous

Criticisms of the AA model are many. It is reported to be highly male-dominated in administration; it makes no provision for the non-religious or atheists; and is historically anti-psychotherapy and anti-medication. In many ways, AA operates in a time vacuum straight from the religious fervor of the 1930s, and has made every attempt to prevent incorporation of new research and new insight into the nature of addictions, and has refused to consider any new approaches to group psychology or individual psychotherapy which have arisen out of the research conducted in the past 65 years.

In fact, AA operates as a closed system, eschewing any injection of newer techniques. AA wants everyone to accept the "disease of alcoholism," according to its definition, yet refuses to accept psychobiological changes in research, such as anti-depressants, which may treat the underlying causes of addiction. Instead, AA sees the "cure" for alcoholism as a moral cure, one based in acceptance of a Christian evangelical religious base, with complete and utter fidelity to the AA way of doing things.

Cathleen A. Mann, April 2003, www.morerevealed.com.

The first of these controlled studies of AA's effectiveness was conducted in San Diego in the mid-1960s. In the study, 301 public drunkenness offenders were randomly divided into three groups. One group was assigned to attend AA, another to attend an alcoholism treatment clinic, and a third group, the control, was not assigned to any treatment program. All of the study's subjects were followed for at least one full year following conviction. Results were calculated by counting the number and frequency of rearrests for drunkenness. Surprisingly, the no-treatment control group was the most successful of the three, with 44% of its members having no rearrests; 32% of those assigned to the clinic group had no rearrests; and 31% of those assigned to AA had no rearrests. As well, 37% of the members of the control group had two or more rearrests, while 40% of the alcoholism clinic attendees were arrested at least two times, and 47% of the AA attendees were arrested at least twice. While far from a definitive debunking of AA's alleged effectiveness, these results are certainly suggestive.

The other controlled study of AA's effectiveness was very carefully designed and conducted, and was carried out in Kentucky in the mid-1970s. A large majority of its subjects were obtained via the court system, and seemed to be "representative of the 'revolving door' alcoholic court cases in our cities." The investigators divided 197 subjects into five randomly selected groups: a control group given no treatment; a group assigned to traditional insight therapy administered by professionals; a group assigned to nonprofessionally led Rational Behavior Therapy (lay RBT);[2] a group assigned to professionally led Rational Behavior Therapy; and a group assigned to AA. Length of treatment varied from 202 to 246 days, and subjects were evaluated at the end of treatment and also at three months and 12 months following its termination.

The AA Group Reported the Most Binges

In general, the groups given professional treatment did better than the nonprofessionally treated groups and the control group. A significant finding, however, was that treatment of any kind was preferable to no treatment.

Since a great many alcohol abusers never seek professional treatment, it's particularly important to compare the results of the AA, lay RBT, and control groups. Lay RBT was clearly superior to AA in terms of dropout rate. During the study, 68.4% of those assigned to AA stopped attending it, while only 40% of those attending lay RBT sessions stopped attending them. Further, at the termination of treatment, all of the lay RBT participants who had persisted in treatment re-

2. Rational Behavior Therapy (RBT) is a short-term, drug-free system of psychotherapy and self-help techniques.

ported that they were drinking less than they were before treatment, while only two-thirds of those who had continued to attend AA reported decreased drinking. As well, during the final three months of treatment, the mean number of arrests was 1.24 for the lay RBT group, 1.67 for the AA group, and 1.79 for the control group.

Perhaps most interestingly, the number of reported binges at three months after termination of treatment was far higher for the AA group than for the lay RBT or control groups. The mean number of reported binges by the AA attendees was 2.37 over the previous three months, while the mean number reported by the controls was 0.56, and the mean for the lay RBT group was only 0.26. This finding strongly suggests that the AA attendees had accepted AA's "one drink, one drunk" dogma, and had then proceeded to "prove" it. It's pertinent to note, however, that at 12 months following the termination of treatment there were no significant differences between the AA, lay RBT, and control groups. One possible interpretation of this finding is that the positive effects of Rational Behavior Therapy fade with time in the absence of continued practice, and that the harmful effects of exposure to AA (at least in regard to bingeing) also fade with time in the absence of further exposure to AA. . . .

AA Is Not Effective

For now, the best evidence available suggests that AA is ineffective as a means of overcoming alcohol problems, and there's some evidence that exposure to AA worsens at least one significant abusive behavior—binge drinking. But the evidence is not conclusive, and until additional controlled studies are conducted, it will remain impossible to draw firm conclusions about AA's (in)effectiveness. One thing, however, bears repeating: *there's no good evidence to indicate that AA is any more effective than "spontaneous recovery."* Assertions that AA is an effective means of overcoming alcohol problems, let alone assertions that AA is the *most* or the *only* effective means of doing so, are just that—assertions, and groundless ones at that.

"The data suggested 'the possibility that . . . some alcoholics can return to moderate drinking with no greater chance of relapse than if they had abstained.'"

Moderate Drinking Is an Effective Treatment for Some Alcoholics

Heather Ogilvie

In the following viewpoint Heather Ogilvie argues that what is called alcoholism is often the result of behavior that the alcoholic can change. In such cases, she asserts, the optimum solution might not be total abstinence but moderate drinking. Further, she contends that alcoholics are better served by being told that they can regain control of their lives by making choices in their own treatment rather than by being told that they have an uncontrollable disease. Heather Ogilvie is the author of *Alternatives to Abstinence: A New Look at Alcoholism and the Choices in Treatment*, from which this viewpoint was adapted.

As you read, consider the following questions:
1. In Heather Ogilvie's opinion, who is responsible for the idea that alcoholism is reversible?
2. What does Heather Ogilvie argue is the correlation between college-age binge drinking and heavy drinking behavior after college?
3. According to the author, who responds best to controlled drinking therapy?

Heather Ogilvie, "Alcoholism: A Different Approach," *Consumers' Research Magazine*, vol. 85, June 2002, pp. 10–13. Copyright © 2001 by Heather Ogilvie. Published by Hatherleigh Press. All rights reserved. Reproduced by permission.

M ost Americans think of problem drinking as the disease of alcoholism. They believe the problem drinker is a sick person who requires treatment. The public is also under the impression that the primary evidence corroborating that a heavy drinker has the disease is his unwillingness to admit it—his denial. Treatments based on the classic disease concept of alcoholism, with its notions of irreversibility and loss of control, prescribe one goal: total abstinence.

Furthermore, when most Americans think of treatment for drinking problems, two things come to mind: 28-day inpatient recovery programs (such as the Betty Ford Center) and the "12 Step" program of Alcoholics Anonymous (AA). There are, however, at least a dozen alternative approaches to treatment that have been proven at least as effective as AA and inpatient programs (most of which are also based on the "12 Steps").

There is also another, strikingly different, concept of treatment that goes sharply counter to the now-traditional disease concept and its total abstinence prescription. This competing view, which has gained adherents in recent years, holds that what is called alcoholism is often a result of modifiable behavior patterns that are within the power of the individual to change, and that in such cases the optimum solution may well be, not total abstinence, but sensible moderation in drinking.

At issue in debates about these matters—and of urgent interest to anyone who must deal with them as they relate to family or friends—is which of these two different approaches is more effective in managing the problem. In some cases it may be one, in some cases it may be the other.

Since its founding in the mid-1930s, the fellowship of AA has undoubtedly saved countless lives. The people who are able to maintain sobriety through AA should certainly continue to attend meetings. But AA does not work for everyone. Various estimates suggest that more than half of the people who attend AA meetings drop out within the first year. Of the people who regularly attend meetings, only about 25% succeed in a goal of long-term abstinence. Most professionals performing alcohol-related research today aim to make available treatment options that can help the problem drinkers for whom AA does not work or does not appeal, as well as for those who never even try AA.

Alcoholism May Be Reversible

Unfortunately, few treatment options have better outcomes than AA: 25% is about the best any one program can boast. This is not great news, as it is estimated that a third of all problem drinkers cut down or quit drinking on their own. To even suggest that some problem drinkers recover on their own is heresy to the advocates of the disease model, as alcoholism is, by their definition, irreversible. They argue that those drinkers who appear to have reduced their drinking to moderate, nonproblematic amounts were never true alcoholics to begin with. This thinking is not particularly helpful, as it makes it impossible to tell a "true" alcoholic from a mere heavy drinker until serious damage has been done. . . .

The idea of the irreversibility of alcoholism has been propagated by Alcoholics Anonymous with such phrases as "Once an alcoholic, always an alcoholic," "always recovering, never recovered," and "one drink, one drunk." Dr. D.L. Davies challenged that notion in his 1962 report that followed up on diagnosed "alcohol addicts" who had been treated in a London hospital seven to 10 years earlier. Dr. Davies noted in his report that seven out of the 93 male patients seemed to be drinking normally.

Nearly 80 studies had been published in the scientific literature prior to 1980, demonstrating that non-problem drinking is a stable treatment outcome. These studies reported rates of observed normal drinking among previously diagnosed alcoholics varying between 2% and 32%. The Rand Corporation assessed data collected from alcoholism treatment centers nationwide between 1970 and 1974, and found that the data suggested "the possibility that for some alcoholics, moderate drinking is not necessarily a prelude to a full relapse and that some alcoholics can return to moderate drinking with no greater chance of relapse than if they had abstained."

Dr. George Vaillant, analyzing data from Harvard Medical School's *Study of Adult Development*—which followed 660 men from 1940 to 1980, from their adolescence into late middle age—found that alcohol abuse among college-age men was a very poor predictor of heavy drinking at middle age. This finding supports other studies that have found that most college-age binge drinkers outgrow their heavy drinking behavior once they leave college and begin jobs or start families. K.M. Fillmore's follow-up of college students with drinking problems found that only 20% still had problems 20 years later. Dr. Vaillant wrote: "The course of alcohol abusers in the college sample contradicted my previous assertions that sustained alcohol abuse without abstinence is a progressive disorder."

Alcoholics Can Control Their Drinking

The notion of loss of control also figures prominently in the classic disease model of alcoholism. Researchers have devised many experiments to assess whether a drinker has indeed experienced a physical loss of control following a "priming dose" of alcohol. An experiment conducted at Johns Hopkins University in 1971 tried to determine the incentives it would take to get an alcoholic not to drink. Researchers found that abstinence could be bought for as little as $7 and no more than $20 a day.

Other studies have replicated this finding. In a five-week experiment, inpatient subjects were given the option to drink up to 10 ounces of alcohol every weekday. Every other week, the subjects were given access to an improved environment—including telephone, television, pool table, games, and reading materials—provided they drank fewer than 5 ounces of alcohol for the day. If the subject exceeded that amount, he was put in a more Spartan environment and was not allowed to drink the following day. On the alternate weeks, the subjects remained in ascetic environments no matter how much they drank. All five subjects drank less during the weeks when privileges were available than during the weeks when no privileges were available.

A 1977 review of scientific literature cited 58 studies that have corroborated the finding that alcoholic drinking is a function of "environmental contingencies.". . .

As the classic disease concept of addiction was eroded by reports of "normal" drinking among previously diagnosed alcoholics, researchers began to wonder whether "normal" or moderate drinking was a viable treatment goal for some alcoholics. The first widely cited report of successful training for controlled drinking appeared in 1970. Researchers applied behavioral therapy techniques in treating 31 alcoholics, after which 24 managed to drink in a "controlled" manner for periods ranging from four months to a little over one year (the length of follow-up). These results sparked an interest among other researchers who were eager to duplicate the study's outcome.

One study compared a controlled-drinking treatment program with one whose goal was abstinence. Roughly one-third of each treatment group was abstinent for a year following treatment. Immediately following treatment, the members of both groups who were not abstinent had cut down to approximately half their pre-treatment alcohol consumption. Three months later, the drinkers in the group trained for abstinence were drinking 70% as much as they had before treatment, while the drinkers in the controlled-drinking group had further reduced their consumption to about 20% of their pre-treatment levels. Over six months' time, the drinkers in the controlled-drinking group continued to reduce their consumption by a greater amount than did those in the abstinence-oriented group.

Controversial Study Promotes Controlled Drinking

The most controversial controlled-drinking study was reported in 1972, by researchers Mark and Linda Sobell. Their 40 volunteer subjects were male inpatients at Patton State Hospital in California. The Sobells treated their controlled-drinking subjects with their own "Individualized Behavior Therapy" (IBT). The Sobells concluded: "[S]ubjects who received the program of . . . IBT with a treatment goal of controlled drinking . . . functioned significantly better throughout the two-year follow-up period than did their respective control subjects . . . who received conventional abstinence-oriented treatment." They also noted: "[O]nly subjects treated by IBT with a goal of controlled drinking successfully engaged in a substantial amount of limited, non-problem drinking during the two years of follow-up, and those subjects also had more abstinent days than subjects in any other group."

Another controlled-drinking study involved randomly dividing 70 problem drinkers, who were each drinking roughly 70 ounces of alcohol per week, into an abstinence group and a controlled-drinking group (whose members were asked to abstain for the first four sessions of treatment). During the first three weeks, the members of the abstinence group drank much more than the controlled-drinking group and significantly more of the controlled-drinking group actually abstained. A year later, no significant difference existed between the groups, but the abstinence group had sought help more frequently than had the controlled drinkers.

Abstinence Is Not the Answer to All Drinking Problems

Dr. Fred Glaser, an expert in addiction medicine at East Carolina University, says the one-size-fits-all abstinence approach to alcoholism—virtually the only method of treatment offered in the United States—may be hurting people's chances for recovery and driving away people who need help. Glaser, who runs a course that teaches problem drinkers to reduce their drinking, says his program appeals to people who might otherwise not seek treatment at all. An approach that advocates controlled drinking, he says, can reach a larger number of alcoholics and is preferable to "trying to shove abstinence goals into everybody who comes in for help with a drinking problem."

Rebecca Raphael, June 7, 2002, ABCnews.com.

Another study of male veterans divided participants into two groups: one receiving abstinence-oriented treatment and the other receiving controlled-drinking treatment. After six months, the severely dependent members of the controlled-drinking group experienced more days of heavy drinking than did those in the abstinence group; however, after one year, the differences disappeared, and at six years there were no significant differences between the two groups.

One might think that controlled-drinking treatment would appeal to every alcoholic, but this is not the case. In one study of 63 alcohol-dependent men given the choice in treatment goals between abstinence and controlled drinking, roughly 70% chose abstinence. Indeed, controlled-drinking studies have shown that most people who moderate their drinking eventually abstain. According to one researcher: "Our long-term follow-up research with clients treated with a moderation goal found that more wound up abstaining than moderating their drinking without problems."

Some Alcoholics Choose Abstinence

Other researchers have reached similar conclusions. In one study, 75% of participants who reported previous drinking problems recovered without formal treatment (i.e., eliminated all problems resulting from overdrinking), and 50% achieved stable, moderate drinking. University of Washington Professor G. Alan Marlatt concludes: "Contrary to the progressive disease model, these findings indicate that a majority of individuals with drinking problems recover on their own . . . Even when they are trained in controlled drinking, many alcohol-dependent individuals choose abstinence. Over time, rates of abstinence (as compared to controlled drinking) tend to increase."

Who responds best to controlled drinking therapy? In general, people under 40 who have suffered less severe dependence-related problems, people with stable marital or family relationships, people with stable employment, and women.

Younger people and those whose problems are not that severe are notoriously difficult to attract into conventional treatment and to persuade to adopt a goal of abstinence. One study found that young, unmarried men with a low level of dependence were 10 times more likely to relapse if they had adopted abstinence as a goal than if they had become moderate, nonproblem drinkers 18 months after treatment. Offering young drinkers the option of controlled-drinking counseling may therefore draw them into treatment sooner and thus prevent them from developing worse drinking problems down the line.

Even in cases in which abstinence is clearly the most pragmatic treatment goal (for example, for a 55-year-old male who has been in and out of detox wards for 35 years), offering the option of moderation may at least bring the person into treatment he might otherwise shun. Once the person is in treatment, a failed attempt at controlled drinking may prove the case for abstinence more persuasively than would a confrontational therapist citing disease-theory dogma for hours on end. As Dr. Marlatt puts it: "From a public health perspective, it makes sense to offer moderation-oriented programs to alcohol abusers and mildly dependent individuals as a means of increasing client recruitment and retention. Individuals who do not benefit from these programs can be 'stepped up' to more intensive abstinence-oriented services.". . .

Patient Control Can Help Recovery

In "12 Step" recovery programs, the client is told (a) his drinking is beyond his control—in fact, he is powerless against it, (b) his condition is irreversible and incurable, and (c) the success of the treatment depends solely on a Higher Power. While that Higher Power may be the god of any religion, the group, or another person, it must be a power other than the individual. A person who prefers to see himself as the effective power, therefore, would not find AA helpful in improving his sense of self-efficacy, his (supposedly absent) self-control, or his will power not to take another drink.

Disease theory proponents argue that attributing the drinker's problems to a disease outside her control frees her from the guilt and stigma of moral weakness. It clears her conscience enough to admit the problem and not be ashamed to seek help.

But doesn't the disease perspective merely swap one stigma—that of moral failing—for another—that of being diseased? By assigning responsibility for the problem to something outside the person, the disease perspective tells him, in effect, that he is powerless and therefore helpless. The person learns to think of himself as a victim.

Stanton Peele, one of the most outspoken critics of conventional addiction treatment, has observed that recovering alcoholics are able to "use their addicted identity to explain all their previous problems without actually doing anything concrete to improve their performance." He accuses traditional treatment of ignoring "the rest of the person's problems in favor of blaming them all on the addiction" and limiting clients' "human contacts primarily to other recovering alcoholics who only reinforce their preoccupation with drinking";

in effect, trapping them "in a world inhabited by fellow disease sufferers" until they "feel comfortable only with others in exactly the same plight."

Wouldn't it be more productive for the drinker to think he has a personality weakness he can overcome, rather than a lifelong disease he can never shake? Might not the shame of a moral failure be put to good use? Some people have wondered: Why shouldn't alcoholics feel ashamed of their behavior? Wouldn't a greater sense of shame have prevented the behavior in the first place?

Few Can Maintain Twelve-Step Sobriety

What good is it to tell someone he is sick and powerless, but then send him to a self-help group, rather than to a doctor, for treatment? In his book, *Heavy Drinking*, Herbert Fingarette asks: "If the alcoholic's ailment is a disease that causes an inability to abstain from drinking, how can a program insist on voluntary abstention as a condition for treatment? (And if alcoholics who enter these programs do voluntarily abstain—as in fact they generally do—then of what value is the [disease] notion of loss of control?)"

The danger of constantly telling people that they have no control is that eventually they may come to believe it. Falling off the wagon thus only proves to the drinker what he has been told: that he has no control. Henceforth, what is his motivation to keep attending AA or to seek further treatment? Treatment professionals who advocate "12 Step" programs typically regard relapse not as a failure of treatment, but as a failure of the patient to comply with treatment. Given these conditions, it is no wonder so few people are able to maintain long-term sobriety through "12 Step" recovery programs.

On the other hand, when you tell someone that, with time and effort, he can change his habits, make improvements to troublesome aspects of his life, and reverse the course of his drinking problems, he will probably be more willing to give treatment a try and recognize the signs of his progress. By showing him he has choices for treatment, you provide more hope and give him back a sense of control simply by allowing him to choose.

*"The goal [of harm reduction] is to move
clients to a more secure footing in life, to
help them to resolve other problems, and to
encourage better health and functioning
generally."*

Reducing the Harm Caused by Drinking Can Be an Effective Treatment

Stanton Peele

Stanton Peele argues in the following viewpoint that while
some alcoholics can never achieve total abstinence, harm reduction is a valuable treatment strategy that can protect
them from the worst consequences of their alcohol abuse.
Further, he contends that brief interventions with a trained
counselor can have a more positive impact on an alcoholic
than months or years of "recovering" in a group setting such
as Alcoholics Anonymous meetings. Stanton Peele, a psychologist and researcher specializing in drug and alcohol addiction, is the author of *The Diseasing of America: How We Allowed Recovery Zealots and the Treatment Industry to Convince
Us We Are Out of Control.*

As you read, consider the following questions:

1. According to Peele, approximately how many alcohol
   dependent individuals enter treatment?
2. In the author's opinion, what is the only treatment
   program officially endorsed in the United States?
3. What does Peele maintain is the underlying basis of
   harm reduction strategy?

Harm reduction is a term best known in the substance abuse field as a way of reforming drug policy. Replacing zero-tolerance policy, it recognizes the certainty that some people will continue to use drugs and therefore that drug use will remain a fact of life in our society. With this in mind, it seeks to protect drug users—and non-drug users exposed to drug users—from the worst consequences of such use. Harm can occur for even casual drug users, but the worst consequences are likely to befall heavy users. In this way, harm reduction is a treatment strategy that may also be appropriate for alcoholics.

Research Results Are Discouraging—and Encouraging

By now it is clear that standard, one-on-one or group addiction therapy in the United States is not sufficiently comprehensive to deal with the range of alcoholism problems facing it. Only about one in four alcohol dependent individuals enters treatment (including AA [Alcoholics Anonymous]) at all, according to the National Alcohol Epidemiologic Survey (NLAES), the largest household survey of Americans' drinking ever conducted. Only a further minority of this proportion seriously engages in available treatments (one rule of thumb derived from AA's biannual surveys is that one in ten of those who come to AA continues to engage for as long as a year).

Moreover, the largest trial of psychotherapy thus far, Project MATCH [Matching Alcoholism Treatments to Client Hetergeneity], was completed in 1996. It produced results that could be disheartening to standard treatment approaches. MATCH—in which treatments were designed by leading practitioners and researchers, with cutting-edge manuals for guidance, for which therapists were carefully trained and closely supervised, and where patients were high-prognosis volunteers—found that few alcoholics abstained for even as long as a year following treatment. MATCH used three treatments (12-step facilitation, coping skills therapy, and motivational enhancement therapy) and two treatment groups—a strictly outpatient group and a group which first underwent hospital treatment. Of the former group, fewer than one in ten (9 percent) abstained throughout the first follow-up year. Of the latter, only about a third (35 percent) did.

Yet, clients seemed to benefit from the treatment. Liver functioning for the group improved and their drinking problems were reduced. Representatives of the government sponsor of the research, NIAAA [National Institute on Alcohol Abuse and Alcoholism], viewed the project and the treatments it included as highly successful. However, in order to do so, the investigators couched the results in nonabstinence terms, pointing out that subjects began treatment averaging 15 drinks on every drinking day, which included 25 days of the month, while after treatment they were drinking on only six days of the month, and having only three drinks per occasion.

One further aspect of Project MATCH that stood out was the minimal amount of therapeutic contact required to produce its results. Twelve-step facilitation and coping skills therapy required only 12 one-hour sessions, while motivation enhancement included only four sessions. Moreover, subjects on average attended only two-thirds of assigned sessions. Motivational enhancement therapy consists of encouraging alcoholics to examine their lives and values and to decide for themselves that, on balance, they want to seek sobriety. This therapy places the weight of decision-making—and also the mechanics of changing drinking habits—on the individual.

In its brevity and the reliance on clients themselves, the motivational enhancement component of Project MATCH resembles brief interventions. These are usually physician-initiated interactions with patients in which doctors provide feedback on the level of a person's drinking, arrive with the patient at goals (usually for reducing rather than quitting drinking), and check up during subsequent office visits on the patient's success at achieving these. Tested in numerous clinical trials, brief interventions have by now shown the greatest success, as measured by research outcomes, of any treatment for drinking problems. At the same time, along with motivation enhancement, they are the least costly counselor-assisted therapies and are highly cost-effective.

While brief interventions are restricted generally to non-dependent drinkers, the Project MATCH population was nearly all alcohol-dependent, and at a fairly high level of dependence. Thus, MATCH suggests that benefits of brief interventions relying on patient initiatives and compliance have greater generalizability. One further aspect of MATCH should be noted in this regard, however. Although there was minimal therapist contact, and especially so in the motivational enhancement therapy component, there was frequent, regular follow-up contact for the purpose of performing research assessments. In other words, subjects knew and anticipated that Project personnel would be in touch with them to see how they were measuring up.

American Treatment Contrasts with the International Movement

The Project MATCH results might have prepared us for the outcome of another year-long assessment announced in the prestigious *New England Journal of Medicine*. Designed to assess the benefits of naltrexone for a highly alcoholic population of veterans, the study instead found *no difference* in outcomes for the group receiving naltrexone for the full year, naltrexone for three months and placebo thereafter, and placebo for the full year. This, after naltrexone had been touted as the first reliable pharmacological therapy for alcohol dependence. Once again, it was not that clients showed no improvement. Combined with unspecified 12-step counseling, the treatments (including placebo) once again produced little abstinence. Nonetheless, while subjects had been drinking on two-thirds of days at the beginning of the year, by the end they had cut their drinking days to one quarter of this frequency, as well as drinking about twenty-five percent less on each drinking day.

The Project MATCH results, at least, occurred with volunteer, non-criminal, socially stable subjects. Yet few of these alcoholics could abstain for even a year following treatment. These outcomes with a propitious population show us that to insist on having patients who desire to abstain—and are capable, or largely so, of abstaining—is to disregard the bulk of alcoholic and drug-abusing patients.

Restricting treatment to those most motivated and able to quit entirely is to select those who actually need therapy the least. Yet this is the principle according to which nearly all treatment is conducted in the U.S.

This treatment landscape in the U.S. contrasts with an international movement in drug policy towards harm reduction. Harm reduction takes as its point of departure that few people quit drugs at any given time, and that, therefore, policies have to be in place for reducing the harms experienced by those who continue to use. One example is clean needle programs, which help prevent the spread of AIDS among IV drug users. Programs which shift drug users to non-injectibles—such as methadone—are based on a similar strategy for preventing worst-case outcomes. Such programs also encourage regular contacts with medical or professional staff that help the user to get treatment for other medical conditions and to preserve their health in other ways.

The concept of harm reduction has taken hold in Europe where, unlike the United States, every national government endorses or provides needle exchange programs. It has had a certain amount of penetration in the U.S. as well. What follows are methods for counselors to deal with addicts and alcoholics which are consistent with the harm reduction ideology. This often involves counselors in whole new ways of thinking about clients and the therapeutic relationship. To the extent that counselors can adopt these tools they often find that they can both improve their outcomes and reach more people.

Harm Reduction Therapy

In the U.S., virtually no treatment program officially endorses—or even tolerates—anything but abstinence. This is emphasized by the virtual universal reliance by treatment programs on AA and related support programs in combination with treatment. In practice, what this means is that clients often drop out of treatment when they realize they are not meeting the total abstinence requirements of the program, or they are judged to be failing since they are not meeting those requirements. Indeed, for a clinician to acknowledge that he or she tolerates drinking by clients would ordinarily mean the counselor will himself or herself be asked to leave the program. At the same time, of course, therapists, even in this environment, make many accommodations for clients who they feel are making a serious effort to change.

The Cycle of Addiction

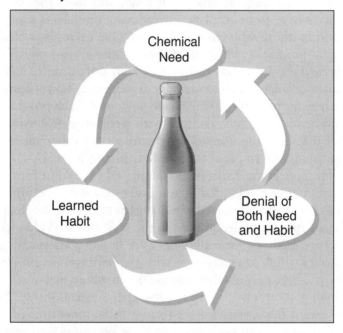

The "cycle of addiction" contains three debilitating elements: chemical need (at the physiological cellular level), learned habit (chronic drinking/using behavior and associations), and denial of both need and habit.

The cycle of alcohol addiction usually develops over a period of years. Cycles have been found to be much shorter with other drugs, especially cocaine. In all cases, however, the addiction becomes "Priority One," a separate issue from everything else. And as it progresses, it begins to negate everything else.

Secular Organizations for Sobriety, February 2, 2002. www.secularsobriety.org.

If a strictly traditional approach had been applied to Project MATCH or the naltrexone trial, subjects might have been rejected as clients, or they would have quit, throughout the course of the treatments and their follow-up. Yet, in both cases, there was broad improvement among the subjects. Moreover, their failure to achieve or adhere to abstinence regimens is, by all indications, typical for alcoholics overall, even those who volunteer for treatment. And, were counselors better able to tolerate failures to abstain, a broader array of patients would be available for treatment, including the very many people who now fall totally outside the treatment net.

What does this mean for counselors? According to the harm reduction approach, the goal is reduction in negative outcomes, and improvement in drinking practices, whether fewer days of drinking (i.e., more abstinence) or fewer drinks (less bingeing) on drinking occasions. Even when drinking, the emphasis is on avoiding risky situations. This notably includes driving. Other such situations include arenas where people may incur criminal penalties, lose a job, engage in violence, and otherwise experience negative outcomes over and above those due purely to the direct effects of drinking.

To take a practical example (one that might admittedly seem scary to many counselors), if a man is unwilling or unable to give up drinking, it could still be highly therapeutic for him to restrict his drinking to his home. In this case, he could avoid confrontations with the law, the possibility of driving and other accidents, and other negative outcomes that can be piled onto his drinking problem to guarantee he can not emerge from their combined weight for decades.

Can . . . a counselor practice such an approach? The answer to this involves a host of individual and situational factors. These include the therapist's tolerance for working in a different fashion from those around him or her, the openness of fellow counselors or of supervisors, the availability of nontraditional therapy outposts, like AIDS-prevention or needle-exchange networks, and many other conditions.

Let us focus in our discussion here on therapeutic techniques and attitudes. Such an approach requires primarily non-judgmental caring. That is, the therapist must convey that he or she is concerned for the patient's well-being, and wants to see improvement. But the therapist then does not conclusively reject the individual who continues to drink, even with problems, and even with serious problems, so long as the client is showing long-range positive movement. Improvement includes not only fewer alcohol-specific problems, but improved relationships with others, performance at work, maintenance of health, etc. The therapist must keep in mind that, after all, if the client leaves the counseling setting altogether, then the counselor has no leverage to encourage and monitor progress.

And, of course, we need to consider what human contact and care even those alcoholics who have currently abandoned hope of improvement may receive.

Learning from Brief Interventions

What is the average counselor to make of the fact that treatments involving a couple of sessions can produce substantial changes in behavior? The idea underlying brief interventions and motivational enhancement is that the counselor acts as a positive force for the individual, and that the relationship continues over time. Frequency is not the primary measure of therapeutic interaction, but duration. It is better to have a bad session or period and to have the client return over time, and to have some contact to reinvest the person in the change effort, than to express disaffection or to censure patients for each negative incident they experience. Indeed, the optimal program is one which has the best chance of guaranteeing that patients will see the counselor again on a voluntary basis.

Keep in mind that the typical brief intervention program occurs within ongoing primary care doctor-patient relationships. Clients then know that they will be held accountable for creating and tracking their own progress, on which they will have to report, and that failures to show progress are strictly their own, although their counselor cares and will learn about it.

Typical counselor comments in this setting include, "John, we meet again in _____ weeks/months, on _____. What goals do we hope to have achieved when we meet again? What do you need to do to make sure these happen? Is there anything I or my agency can provide to help you do this? What are the signs we are looking for to see that you have made the progress we hope for? John, I may call you some time—maybe more than once—before you return, to chat with you about how you are doing and to make sure we are on track. Do you mind? Or, how about if you call me for a quick chat? John, I want you to know I have great confidence in you to make the changes we discussed. I know you have had some problems in your life, but you have also had many successes that we have discussed. And I know that when you set out to change something in your life, you can do so. I'll bet on it."

Of course, even when John is not showing progress, there is a need to remain in contact with him, to show that we remain concerned. Sometimes, remarkably, at some point in the future, John will show up ready and able to do those things that he seems incapable of now.

But harm reduction extends beyond the issue of the drinking and drug use in which the the individual is engaging. The goal is to move clients to a more secure footing in life, to help them to resolve other problems, and to encourage better health and functioning generally. Thus, the harm reduction counselor is highly attuned to other needs clients have, and to the possibility they can be referred beneficially to other health professionals, social service agencies, et al. The underlying thinking is that the more socially stable, healthy, and productive people can be, the better decisions they will make about their substance use. And, in any case, their lives and health can be made better even in the absence of distinct reductions, or cessation of, substance use and abuse.

Tolerance Can Be a Powerful Therapeutic Tool

Among other things, the image of addiction treatment and counseling may need to change. Now, counselors typically see themselves like a latter-day Mother Teresa. At least, they feel that responsibility for change is on their shoulders. Therapists might assume more humility. Like the parent who has no emotional outlet but his or her children, the danger is that the clucking chicken will be so invested in the outcomes of his or her charges that they will never learn to function for themselves at whatever level they can ultimately achieve. Lack of perfection in a client—like lack of perfection in ourselves—is to be expected. This is not to gainsay the chance for something better for all of us. But it is to take tolerance as a powerful therapeutic tool. Perhaps some time in the future there will be something superior to naltrexone in the way of a pharmacotherapy for addiction. But there will always be room for the enterprise of encouraging the halting, imperfect improvement of the human species.

*"Currently available drugs are seldom the
total answer for the alcoholic in search of
sobriety—but in at least some cases, they
can be of enormous assistance."*

Medication May Help
Alcoholics Stay Sober

Behavior Medical Associates

Drug therapy can help alcoholics fight cravings and
strengthen their resolve not to drink, argue experts at Behavior Medical Associates, a private outpatient mental
health practice in Atlanta, Georgia. They contend that any
length of time an alcoholic can go without a drink allows his
or her psychological and physiological processes to begin to
return to normal. Drugs such as Antabuse cause alcoholics
to vomit if they consume alcohol and thus strengthens their
determination not to drink. Other medications can reduce
an alcoholic's craving for alcohol and can be especially helpful during the early stages of sobriety, the experts claim.

As you read, consider the following questions:
1. What do the authors argue will happen to an alcoholic's
   craving for alcohol after he or she has been sober for a
   while?
2. According to the authors, why is Antabuse not more
   widely used?
3. In the authors' opinion, what does the future hold for
   drug therapy for alcoholism?

Although the obvious treatment for alcoholism—*just don't drink the alcohol!*—seems and in fact is quite simple in theory, it is by no means easy in practice for individuals with the medical illness of alcohol dependence.

The abnormal craving and mental obsession alcoholics have for alcohol causes them to return to it again and again even when their drinking has repeatedly caused terrible problems for themselves and others. Even when they finally reach the stage at which they genuinely want to stop drinking, many alcoholics find abstinence from alcohol difficult or impossible to achieve or to maintain. They may stop for a while only to resume drinking again later, usually with a recurrence of problems followed by another, often unsuccessful attempt to stop and stay stopped drinking. Mark Twain said that "It's easy to quit smoking—I've done it a hundred times." The same applies to alcoholics who stop drinking. Many, in fact most will stop drinking. But relatively few will be successful in staying stopped for a significant period of time. And length of time without a drink is very important for the alcoholic's recovery because time is required for his psychological and physiological (biochemical) processes to begin to return to normal.

Anything that assists the alcoholic in refraining from drinking alcohol, therefore, permits his natural bodily and mental functions to reassert themselves after the deformations caused in them by his prolonged drinking. The longer he goes without a drink the more normal his system becomes. After a while most alcoholics no longer crave and never even think about alcohol—unless they drink it and commence the pathological craving and obsession all over again.

Antabuse (disulfiram) has been available for many years as an adjunct to alcoholism treatment. This medication has no effect on the desire to drink but causes severe sickness if alcohol is consumed while one is taking it. Alcoholics who take Antabuse daily know that if they drink they will get sick (vomiting), hence get a boost in the determination to stay sober. The obvious problem and the reason that Antabuse is not more generally effective than it has been is that alcoholics can simply stop taking the drug and start drinking again after a certain period of time (but not right away—Antabuse blocks drinking for quite a while after the last pill is taken). But Antabuse can provide good protection against momentary and overwhelming urges to drink in alcoholics who are otherwise very determined to stay sober.

Drugs Can Help Diminish the Craving for Alcohol

Other medications such as Revia (naltrexone) and acamprosate do not cause sickness if alcohol is consumed while they are being taken but instead diminish the craving for alcohol and the pleasurable effects from drinking it. Scientific studies show that alcoholics in early recovery who are receiving the standard treatment for alcoholism (counseling, group therapy, AA & etc.) and who are taking these agents along with it are somewhat more successful in staying sober than those who are not. The effect, while real, is not huge. But in a disorder as devastating and difficult to treat as alcoholism, every advantage that can be gained for sobriety is worth using.

When other disorders besides alcoholism (depression, bipolar disorder, anxiety, schizophrenia & etc.) are present along with alcoholism, appropriate drug treatment of these conditions is necessary lest they interfere with the recovery from alcoholism. However, successful treatment of such associated ("dual diagnosis") psychiatric conditions does not itself directly affect the alcoholism, which is a separate medical condition usually requiring separate medical treatment. . . .

It is very likely that new and better drugs will be available in the near future—and that a truly effective treatment for alcoholism will become available that will make its control possible on a much wider scale than ever before.

Meanwhile, alcoholics who get and stay sober usually have to do it "the old fashioned way," namely (1) don't drink the alcohol (one day at a time!), and (2) go to AA meetings. Currently available drugs are seldom the total answer for the alcoholic in search of sobriety—but in at least some cases, they can be of enormous assistance.

Periodical Bibliography

The following articles have been selected to supplement the diverse views presented in this chapter.

Jerry Dorsman	"Can We Still Make a Choice?" *Professional Counselor*, February 2000.
Don H.	"The Damaged Ones Like Me," *World*, January/February 2000.
Thomas R. Hobbs	"Managing Alcoholism as a Disease," *Physician's News Digest*, February 1998.
Linda Davis Kyle	"Alternative Treatments for Addictions: Promises and Perils," *Professional Counselor*, August 1999.
Lance P. Longo and Michael J. Bohn	"Alcoholism Pharmacotherapy: New Approaches to an Old Disease," *Hospital Physician*, June 2001.
Ilana Mercer	"Addictions Are About Behavior, Not Disease," *Calgary Herald*, June 22, 2000.
National Council on Alcoholism and Drug Dependence	"The Disease of Alcoholism," 2002. www.ncadd.org.
National Institute on Alcohol Abuse and Alcoholism	"Alcohol Alert," October 2000. www.niaaa.nih.gov.
David L. Ohlms	"The Disease of Alcoholism," 2002. www.webtree.ca.
Rebecca Raphael	"New Roads to Sobriety: A Controversial Look at Alcohol Abuse and Treatment," June 7, 2002. www.abcnews.com.
Richard A. Rawson et al.	"Pharmacotherapies for Substance-Abuse Treatment: The Beginning of a New Era," *Counselor*, October 2000.
Jeff Sandoz	"The Spiritual Secret to Alcoholism Recovery," *Annals of the American Psychotherapy Association*, September/October 2001.
Devin Sexson	"Mind Control Tactics of Alcoholics Anonymous," June 2002. www.morerevealed.com.
Gerald D. Shulman	"Addiction Treatment 'Success' Is Killing Us," *Behavioral Health Management*, September/October 2002.
Robert M. Swift	"Medications and Alcohol Craving," *Alcohol Research and Health*, March 1999.

CHAPTER 4

What Measures Should Be Taken to Reduce Alcohol-Related Problems?

Chapter Preface

In 1979 a Maryland woman and her infant daughter were involved in a head-on collusion with a drunk driver—a repeat offender with two previous convictions. While Cindi Lamb and her five-and-a-half-month-old daughter Laura survived the accident, Laura was left a quadriplegic. With the help of sympathetic friends, Cindi Lamb began battling drunk driving with public awareness campaigns and efforts to strengthen drunk driving laws in her home state. A year later in California, Candace Lightner's thirteen-year-old daughter Cari was killed by a drunk driver. Like the driver who injured Laura Lamb, Cari's killer was a repeat offender. Fueled by grief at her daughter's senseless death and anger at the lenient laws that allowed a driver with multiple drunk driving convictions to hold a valid driver's license, Lightner joined with other outraged citizens and founded Mothers Against Drunk Drivers (MADD) in Sacramento, California. Lamb soon joined Lightner's fledgling group and created a MADD chapter in Maryland.

By the end of 1981 there were eleven MADD chapters in four states. The organization grew rapidly—by the fall of 1982, there were more than seventy MADD chapters, and at year's end there were a hundred. Most of the chapters were started by victims of drunk driving accidents, who, like Lamb and Lightner, were searching for a way to stop drunk drivers and create something positive out of the tragedy they had experienced. Joining with other like-minded individuals and starting a new MADD chapter offered them an opportunity to help reduce one of the nation's major alcohol-related problems—the scourge of drunk driving.

In 1984 MADD changed its name from Mothers Against Drunk Drivers to Mothers Against Drunk Driving—a change brought about by a shift in the group's focus. MADD was no longer concentrating on the drunk driver as a criminal, but on the act of drunk driving itself. The organization's mission statement was condensed into a simple, powerful message: "To stop drunk driving and to support victims of this violent crime." By its tenth anniversary, MADD had 407 chapters in the United States and other nations. A Gallup poll taken in the early 1990s showed the effectiveness of MADD's campaigning—Americans were more aware of the dangers of drunk driving than ever before and considered it the number one problem on U.S. highways. MADD's growth continued, and by 2000, there were six hundred chapters nationwide and affiliates in Guam, Canada, and Puerto Rico.

The grassroots activism that began with Cindi Lamb and Candace Lightner's tragedies resulted in thousands of saved lives and the passage of a substantial number of federal and state anti–drunk driving laws, MADD supporters maintain. Critics, however, think the organization has gone too far in its relentless war against drunk driving. Cofounder Lightner left MADD in 1998 because she thought the organization had become "overzealous" in the pursuit of its goals, particularly pressuring states to adopt the .08 percent BAC law (the blood alcohol concentration level at which a person is considered legally drunk). H. Laurence Ross, a professor at the University of New Mexico and author of the book, *Confronting Drunk Driving*, argues that MADD's reasons for fighting for a universal .08 BAC law go beyond reducing alcohol-related traffic fatalities. While he doubts that there would be a corresponding decrease in either fatality or accident rates, Ross maintains that a stricter BAC law would result in more arrests for drunk driving, and thus make MADD's campaigns appear successful. Consequently, "for MADD, that would justify more lobbying, more contributions, more PR campaigns, more business for itself," he claims. Critics insist that MADD is one of the most powerful, well-funded, and successful lobbying groups in the country, with a cash flow of $45.5 million in 1994. For this success to continue, according to some critics, the battle against drunk driving can never appear to be won. "I worry that the movement I helped create has lost direction," Lightner said.

Reducing drunk driving and helping drunk driving victims—MADD's mission—is just one approach to reducing alcohol-related problems. Authors in the following chapter debate other solutions as well, such as enacting .08 BAC laws and maintaining a minimum drinking age.

"Studies have consistently shown that .08 BAC laws are associated with reductions in alcohol-related fatalities."

Lowering Blood Alcohol Limits Will Help Prevent Drunk Driving

National Highway Traffic Safety Administration

With a .08 percent blood alcohol concentration (BAC), almost all drivers are impaired, according to the National Highway Traffic Safety Administration (NHTSA) in the following viewpoint. Because of this loss of ability to perform critical driving tasks, the NHTSA argues that all states should make .08 BAC the legal level for drunk driving. The administration contends that states that have enacted a .08 BAC law are experiencing a significant reduction in fatal accidents involving alcohol. NHTSA is part of the U.S. Department of Transportation and is responsible for carrying out motor vehicle safety programs.

As you read, consider the following questions:
1. According to the NHTSA, which group shows the greatest impairment at .08 BAC?
2. What percentage decline in the number of drinking drivers involved in fatal crashes occurred after a .08 BAC law was enacted in Illinois in 1997, according to a 2000 NHTSA study?
3. Why does the NHTSA argue that drunk driving "accidents" do not exist?

National Highway Traffic Safety Administration, "The Case for .08 BAC Laws," *Settings Limits, Saving Lives*, April 2001.

The research is clear. Virtually all drivers are significantly impaired at .08 BAC [blood alcohol concentration]. A 1988 NHTSA [National Highway Traffic Safety Administration] review of 177 studies documented this impairment. In 2000 NHTSA released a review of 112 more recent studies which provided additional evidence of impairment at .08 BAC. Thus, nearly 300 studies have shown that, at .08 BAC, virtually all drivers are impaired with regard to critical driving tasks such as divided attention, complex reaction time, steering, lane changing and judgement.

A new comprehensive laboratory study provides what is perhaps the clearest laboratory evidence to date of the significant impairment that exists in all measures of performance by .08 BAC. In addition, this study finds that impairment exists in relatively equal levels among all age groups, sexes, and drinker types. This study, which employed a driving simulator and special divided attention test was conducted by the Southern California Research Institute, Human Factors North, and Westat Inc., all well-respected firms in the traffic safety research community.

Another reason for supporting .08 BAC laws is because they are effective in reducing alcohol-related fatal crashes. At least nine independent studies have now been conducted, covering nearly all of the states that have enacted .08 BAC laws. These studies have consistently shown that .08 BAC laws are associated with reductions in alcohol-related fatalities, particularly in conjunction with ALR[1] [Administrative License Revocation] laws, already in place in 40 states. . . .

In 1999, NHTSA released three comprehensive studies on the effectiveness of .08 BAC laws. These studies found persuasive evidence that .08 BAC laws are associated with alcohol-related fatal crashes.

Another study was released in 2000 by a Boston University research group. This study found an overall 6 percent

---

1. ALR laws require automatic on-the-spot suspension of the driver's license of a suspected drunk driver who fails, or refuses to take, a chemical or breath sobriety test to determine blood alcohol concentration (BAC). The motorist is issued a temporary driving permit typically valid for 20 to 30 days and is guaranteed an administrative appeal hearing within this time period to contest the revocation.

impact of the laws in six states which enacted .08 BAC laws in 1993 and 1994.

In September 2000, NHTSA released a study on the effectiveness of the .08 BAC law implemented in Illinois in 1997. This study found that the new law was associated with a 13.7 percent decline in the number of drinking drivers involved in fatal crashes. The reduction included drivers at both high and low BAC levels. This is significant because critics of .08 BAC laws have often claimed that they do nothing to affect high BAC drivers. The study also found that there were no major problems reported by law enforcement or sanctioning systems.

A 1999 report by the Government Accounting Office (GAO) reviewed the studies available at that time and found strong indications that .08 BAC laws, in combination with other drunk driving laws (particularly license revocation laws), sustained public education and information efforts, and vigorous and consistent enforcement, can save lives.

An independent, non-federal, Task Force on Community Preventive Services, supported by the Department of Health and Human Services has completed a systematic review of studies of BAC laws. The Task Force unanimously agreed that the evidence for the effectiveness of .08 legislation is strong. The review found that .08 BAC laws consistently resulted in declines in crash fatalities in states in which they were implemented. This in-depth review found a median (7 percent) decline in measures related to alcohol-related fatalities associated with these laws.

Impaired Driving Affects Everyone

About two out of every five Americans will be involved in an alcohol-related crash at some time in their lives, and many of them will be innocent victims. There is no such thing as a drunk driving accident. Virtually all crashes involving alcohol could have been avoided if the impaired person were sober.

As BAC levels rise, so does the risk of being involved in a fatal crash. Recent research has shown that, in single vehicle fatal crashes, the relative fatality risk for drivers with BACs between .08 and .10 is at least eleven times greater than for drivers with a BAC of zero and is 52 times greater for young males. . . .

In the United States, BAC limits are set by states. The limit of .10 found in most states is the highest in the industrialized world.

BAC Is Considered Physical Evidence

The Supreme Court has ruled in *Smerber vs. California* that if an officer has probable cause to believe that a driver is over the legal limit, a BAC test may be conducted by force if necessary. This is because the amount of alcohol in the blood is "physical" evidence like a finger print and not testimonial in nature and therefore is not protected by the Fifth Amendment.

Robert B. Voas, *Washington Post Weekly Edition*, December 13, 1999.

An eleven-state study also examined the effects of .08 BAC and ALR laws. It found that .08 BAC legislation was associated with reductions in alcohol-related fatalities, alone or in conjunction with ALR laws, in seven of the eleven states studied. In five of these states (Vermont, Kansas, North Carolina, Florida, and New Mexico), implementation of the .08 BAC law itself was associated with significantly lower rates of alcohol-related fatalities. These results take into account any pre-existing downward trends the states were already experiencing, due to other factors such as the presence of other laws, use of sobriety checkpoints, etc. In two states (California and Virginia), significant reductions were associated with the combination of .08 BAC and ALR laws, implemented within 6 months of each other. This study also found evidence of reduced alcohol (beer) consumption in several states following implementation of .08 laws.

.08 BAC Laws Have Wide Support

Another study analyzed the effects of a .08 BAC law implemented in 1993 in North Carolina, a state which had already been experiencing a sharp decline in alcohol-related fatalities since 1987. This study concluded that there was little clear effect of the lower BAC limit. Results from various analyses suggested that some reductions may have been associated with the law but the magnitude of these effects was not sufficient to make this conclusion.

NHTSA, the federal agency charged with the safety of motor vehicles and our nation's highway safety, has long supported .08 state laws. In a 1992 *Report to Congress*, the agency recommended that all states lower their illegal *per se* limit to .08 for all drivers 21 years and above. (NHTSA supports zero tolerance for drivers under the legal drinking age.) Numerous other federal agencies with an interest in public health and safety issues, as well as dozens of private sector organizations, support NHTSA's call for universal .08 state laws.

BAC Levels in Other Countries

Austria	.08
Australia	.05
Canada	.08
Finland	.05
United Kingdom	.08
Netherlands	.05
Norway	.05
Sweden	.02
Switzerland	.08

Research by NHTSA, the Boston University School of Public Health, and the California Department of Motor Vehicles have shown impaired driving reductions already attributable to .08, as well as the potential for saving additional lives when all states adopt .08 BAC laws. Not only would deaths and injuries go down, but costs would decline as well. Alcohol-related crashes cost society $45 billion every year, not including pain, suffering, and lost quality of life.

> "*The* . . . New England Journal of Medicine *described driving while talking on a cell phone as a greater impairment than driving at .08 percent BAC.*"

Lowering Blood Alcohol Limits Will Not Help Prevent Drunk Driving

Rick Berman

Hard-core alcohol abusers whose binges result in blood alcohol concentrations (BAC) far in excess of .08 percent cause the majority of alcohol-related traffic fatalities, Rick Berman argues in the following viewpoint. He maintains, therefore, that encouraging states to enact laws that set drunk driving arrest thresholds at .08 is misguided. Such laws will hurt the responsible social drinker who is not impaired with a .08 BAC and does not solve the problem of drunk drivers who cause accidents. Rick Berman is general counsel for the American Beverage Institute.

As you read, consider the following questions:

1. According to the author, what is the focus of the calls for solutions to the problem of drunk driving?
2. In Rick Berman's opinion, which three groups were responsible for the early successes in the fight against drunk driving?
3. Rick Berman argues that MADD's slogan used to be "Don't Drive Drunk." What is the organization's new slogan?

The debate over arresting drinkers who drive is no longer about facts. It's about creating perceptions. Rather than arriving at real solutions to alcohol abuse, the debate has evolved (degraded?) to who should define the problem. . . .

Calls for "solutions" are focused on tighter arrest levels for social drinkers. The problem of alcohol abuse gets little new attention. Is it time for MADD [Mothers Against Drunk Driving] and others to show a willingness to recognize both their past victories and that part of the problem that needs a fresh approach?

The *New York Times* reported [in 1997] that,

> the long national campaign against drunken driving has persuaded some drivers to drink less or not at all. But two recent studies suggest that the people heeding the message are not the ones who drink the most. The studies also hint that may be time for some states and judges to try new strategies.

There is very little left to squeeze out of the 1980's DWI [Driving While Impaired] campaign of "awareness and punishment." Social drinkers know well the dangers of drunk driving. The "one too many" crowd is sufficiently fearful of the punishment for being caught above the legal limit. They have modified their behavior, and the alcohol-related death rates of the '80s dropped accordingly.

Despite those victories however, the decline has reached a point of diminishing returns. We are not reaching the remaining "hard core of alcoholics who do not respond to public appeal," correctly identified by Katherine Prescott, the past president of MADD, because we are not targeting the root cause of the drunk driving problem—alcohol abusers who drive.

It is also well understood that alcoholics cannot be threatened out of their behavior. Alcoholism is a disease that needs more than punishment; intervention and treatment must be part of the solution. We need to employ more compassion and less contempt. Understandably, it's not a mindset that comes easily to victims.

Abusive Drinkers Are the Problem

Our long-running national campaign to combat drunk driving ignores these core dynamics. The typical number of drinks consumed by a 180-pound male associated with a DWI fatality? Ten! A beer every 12 minutes for two hours! And that's an average. Many drink far in excess of that number. That's not "social" by any standard. Yet, the teeth gnashing and press conferences are all about passing new laws to arrest and jail the more responsible adult who chooses to drink moderately before driving.

The Effectiveness of .08 BAC Laws Has Not Been Proven

While indications are that .08 BAC laws in combination with other drunk driving laws as well as sustained public education and information efforts and strong enforcement can be effective, the evidence does not conclusively establish that .08 BAC laws by themselves result in reductions in the number and severity of crashes involving alcohol. Until recently, limited published evidence existed on the effectiveness of .08 BAC laws, and NHTSA's [National Highway Traffic Safety Administration] position—that this evidence was conclusive—was overstated. In 1999, more comprehensive studies have been published that show many positive results, and NHTSA's characterization of the results has been more balanced. Nevertheless, these studies fall short of providing conclusive evidence that .08 BAC laws by themselves have been responsible for reductions in fatal crashes.

U.S. General Accounting Office, June 1999. www.gao.gov.

It wasn't always this way. In the early days in the fight against drunk driving, MADD, the hospitality industry and law enforcement marched lock step in a campaign against drunk driving. The issue of how to address this hard core of alcoholics has since split our united front.

Retailers have not just recently gotten religion on this issue. In 1993, we testified before the House Judiciary Committee and proposed solutions that focused on the still intractable part of the problem—the alcohol abuser. Anti-drinking groups (including many MADD chapters) ignored our suggested focus. It was drinking and driving they were after. And the amount of drinks was not in issue.

To advance their social-drinker focus, MADD and other anti-alcohol activists have changed their mantra from "Don't

Drive Drunk" to "Don't Drink and Drive" to include the responsible social drinker. And according to MADD "Not One Drink" is the standard.

MADD Promotes .08 BAC

The MADD agenda unequivocally argues for a .08 percent BAC (blood alcohol concentration) drunk driving arrest threshold with lower levels to follow. The .08 percent BAC threshold would make it illegal for a 120-pound woman to drink two six-ounce glasses of wine over a two-hour period. (This calculation is straight from a 1998 National Highway Traffic Safety Administration publication.) Not many would suggest this is alcohol abuse.

In response, the "anti" side offers a 4-to-5-beers-in-an-hour scenario to prove their .08 case. Yet this mythical abuser is thin gruel when it comes to real-life examples. Someone who drinks a full beer every 12 minutes will not quit after 60 minutes. This rapid-fire drinking pattern is that of the alcoholic. This mythical .08 drinker will be at that level for only a moment while on his way to a much more dangerous level before reaching for the keys.

But lay aside the debate over two or four drinks and ask: "What exactly is the magic behind this .08 number?" To add some perspective, the respected *New England Journal of Medicine* described driving while talking on a cell phone as a greater impairment than driving at .08 percent BAC. If traffic safety (not alcohol) is really the issue, where is the MADD agenda for jailing those cell phone users? Where are the outraged anti-cell phone Senators who were on the .08 jihad [in 1998]?

Lowering the arrest threshold to .08 percent in an effort to change the behavior of an alcohol abuser with an average BAC double that level is intuitively off base. It is not unlike lowering the speed limit from 60 mph to 50 mph in order to slow down maniacs who drive at 100 mph. Common sense says it won't work.

Of course some need more convincing. To accommodate, [in June 1999] the General Accounting Office shattered the .08 campaign. It reported to Congress that the Boston University research study cited ad nauseam by the .08 proponents was in a word "unfounded." The GAO indicted the National Highway Traffic Safety Administration as well for "overstating" conclusions from their own studies that their underlying research failed to support.

It is understandable that feelings run high in the debate over how to reduce drunk driving. But it is common wisdom that when you allow a fight over the perfect to crowd out implementation of the good, nobody wins—except those addicted to fighting.

*"Compared with . . . other programs . . .
to reduce drinking among teenagers,
increasing the legal age for purchase and
consumption of alcohol to 21 appears to have
been the most successful effort to date."*

Minimum Drinking-Age Laws Are Effective

Alexander C. Wagenaar and Traci L. Toomey

Underage drinking is a serious national problem with substantial social and economic consequences. Alexander C. Wagenaar and Traci L. Toomey argue in the following viewpoint that the establishment of a minimum legal drinking age (MLDA) of twenty-one represents the single most effective approach to curbing underage drinking. They maintain that the age-21 MLDA has saved over seventeen thousand lives since 1975 and could be even more beneficial if it was strictly enforced. Alexander C. Wagenaar and Traci L. Toomey are researchers in the division of epidemiology of the School of Public Health at the University of Minnesota.

As you read, consider the following questions:
1. According to the authors, when did most states establish an MLDA of twenty-one?
2. What penalty did states suffer if they did not raise their MLDA to twenty-one when the federal government enacted the Uniform Drinking Age Act in 1984, according to Wagenaar and Toomey?

Alexander C. Wagenaar and Traci L. Toomey, "Effects of Minimum Drinking Age Laws: Review and Analysis of the Literature from 1960 to 2000," *Journal of Studies on Alcohol*, vol. 63, March 2002, pp. 206–26. Copyright © 2002 by Alcohol Research Documentation, Inc., Rutgers Center of Alcohol Studies, Piscataway, NJ 08854. Reproduced by permission.

The minimum legal drinking age (MLDA) is the most well-studied alcohol control policy in the United States. The intention of this policy is to lower alcohol use and its associated problems among youth. Following Prohibition, most states established an age 21 MLDA. During the early 1970s, a trend toward lowering the MLDA to age 18, 19 or 20 began in the United States, providing many natural experiments. As a result of research evidence indicating that traffic crashes among youth increased following lowering of the legal age, a citizens' effort began urging states to raise the MLDA back to age 21. In 1984, the federal government enacted the Uniform Drinking Age Act, which provided for the withholding of federal highway funds from states that failed to increase their MLDA. By 1988, all states had established an age-21 MLDA. The increase in MLDA across multiple states again provided researchers with many natural experiments to assess effects of these policy changes on alcohol consumption and related problems among youth. . . .

Compared with a wide range of other programs and efforts to reduce drinking among teenagers, increasing the legal age for purchase and consumption of alcohol to 21 appears to have been the most successful effort to date. . . . The magnitude of effects of the age-21 policy may appear small, particularly in studies using weak research designs and having low levels of statistical power. However, even modest effects applied to the entire population of youth result in very large societal benefits. For example, the National Highway Traffic Safety Administration, using an average estimated reduction in traffic fatalities due to the legal drinking age of 13%, calculates that the age-21 policy prevented 846 deaths in 1997 and prevented a total of 17,359 deaths since 1975.

A large proportion of studies of the MLDA found a statistically significant, inverse relationship between the MLDA and alcohol consumption and alcohol-related problems (48% of the higher quality studies). Only a small number of studies found a statistically significant, positive relationship between the MLDA and various outcomes (1% of the higher quality studies). A large number of studies found no statistically significant relationship. In addition to differences in quality of research design and analyses, several other factors

Percent of 10th Grade Girls and Boys Who Binge Drink

	1991	1993	1995	1997	1999
Boys	31.4	27.2	32.1	32.7	33.5
Girls	22.4	25.3	28.3	26.3	31.1

"Youth Risk Behavior Survey," National Center on Addiction and Substance Abuse at Columbia University, February 2002.

may account for variability in results across studies, including size of sample and extent of change in policy. The power to detect a statistically significant effect is directly influenced by the size of the sample. In some states, the MLDA was raised only 1 year, from age 20 to age 21; in other states it was raised from age 18 to 21. Studies of policy changes that affect smaller segments of the population may be less likely to detect effects simply because of reduced statistical power when analyzing fewer data. Given potential design and analysis limitations in any single study, the large proportion of MLDA studies that found a significant inverse relationship with various outcomes gives strong support for the effectiveness of the MLDA.

Strict Enforcement of the MLDA Would Save More Lives

It is difficult to estimate accurately the effects of the drinking age specifically on college students. Unfortunately, most studies focusing on college students have been based on weaker cross-sectional designs or limited nonprobability samples. Only 9% of the college-specific studies (6 of 64) used a higher quality research design. Of these higher quality studies, none found a statistically significant inverse relationship between the MLDA and consumption or alcohol-related problems. In addition, of these 6 analyses, 4 included a sample of students at only one university. Although it is possible that the age-21 policy has been less effective on college campuses than among the general youth population, existing research clearly does not suggest that the age-21 MLDA has increased problems among college students. However, more studies that use robust research designs would be needed to assess accurately the effect of the MLDA specifically on college campuses. In addition, studies of potential mediating factors on campuses are also needed. For example, how well are MLDA laws enforced on college campuses? How easily can underage students obtain alcohol on and around campus? If one assumes that the MLDA is less effective on college campuses, perhaps it is due to lax enforcement and particularly easy access to alcohol by underage youth in such settings.

Finally, despite progress in recent decades, most youth continue to have access to alcohol, most drink at least occasionally, and a substantial fraction regularly become intoxicated. The social costs from injuries, deaths and damage associated with underage drinking remain high. The benefits of the legal drinking age of 21 have occurred with little or no active enforcement in most areas. Simply by increasing enforcement levels and deterring adults from selling or providing alcohol to minors, even more injuries and deaths related to alcohol use among youth are likely to be prevented each year.

"Neo-prohibitionists of today typically argue that raising the drinking age to 21 has been beneficial. However, the evidence suggests a different story."

Minimum Drinking-Age Laws Are Ineffective

David J. Hanson

The minimum drinking age of twenty-one is based on the ideology of prohibitionism rather than on any scientific evidence of its effectiveness, David J. Hanson argues in the following viewpoint. In fact, Hanson contends that major scientific studies offer proof of the ineffectiveness of minimum age drinking laws. Further, he maintains that teaching young people how to drink moderately and responsibly is a better solution to under-age drinking problems than prohibiting them from drinking at all. David J. Hanson is a professor of sociology at the State University of New York at Potsdam.

As you read, consider the following questions:

1. According to Hanson, why have prohibitionists tried to retain their control over the drinking behavior of young people?
2. What does Hanson argue is the impact of raised minimum age legislation on drinking behavior?
3. In Hanson's opinion, what is true about the way the vast majority of drinkers handle alcohol?

Underlying minimum age legislation are the assumptions of American prohibitionism: alcohol consumption is undesirable and dangerous; it typically results in problem behavior; and drinking in any degree is equally undesirable because moderate social drinking is the forerunner of chronic inebriation. Naturally, young people, if not everyone, should be protected from alcohol, according to this view. However, following the repeal of the Eighteenth Amendment in 1933, prohibition efforts have largely been age-specific. While repeal abolished Prohibition in general, prohibitionists have tried to maintain their hold over young people. "The youngest age group is . . . chosen as a symbolic gesture because of its political impotence and because . . . there are not major economic consequences. . ." And there have been no political consequences; young people tend not to vote or otherwise hold politicians accountable for their actions.

Neo-prohibitionists of today typically argue that raising the drinking age to 21 has been beneficial. However, the evidence suggests a different story. For example, a study of a large sample of young people between the ages of 16 and 19 in Massachusetts and New York after Massachusetts raised its drinking age revealed that the average, self-reported daily alcohol consumption in Massachusetts did not decline in comparison with New York. Comparison of college students attending schools in states that had maintained, for a period of at least ten years, a minimum drinking age of 21 with those in states that had similarly maintained minimum drinking ages below 21 revealed few differences in drinking problems. A study of all 50 states and the District of Columbia found "a positive relationship between the purchase age and single-vehicle fatalities." Thus, single-vehicle fatalities were found to be more frequent in those states with high purchase ages.

Comparisons of drinking before and after the passage of raised minimum age legislation have generally revealed little impact upon behavior. For example, a study that examined college students' drinking behavior before and after an increase in the minimum legal drinking age from 18 to 19 in New York State found the law to have no impact on underage students' consumption rates, intoxication, drinking attitudes or drinking problems. These findings were corroborated by other researchers at a different college in the same state. A similar study at Texas A & M University examined the impact of an increase in consumption on alcohol problems among under-age students. However, there was a significant increase among such students in attendance at events where alcohol was present. There were also significant increases in the frequency of their requests to legal-age students to provide alcohol and in their receipt of illicit alcohol from legal-age students.

Increasing the Minimum Drinking Age Causes More Problems

A longitudinal study of the effect of a one-year increase of the drinking age in the province of Ontario [Canada] found that it had a minimum effect on consumption among 18- and 19-year-old high school students and none among those who drank once a week or more. A similar study was conducted among college students in the State University System of Florida to examine their behavior before and after an increase in the drinking age from 19 to 21. While there was a general trend toward reduced consumption of alcohol after the change in law, alcohol-related problems increased significantly. Surveys at Arizona State University before and after that state raised the legal drinking age from 19 to 21 found no reduction in alcohol consumption. Finally, an examination of East Carolina University students' intentions regarding their behavior following passage of the 21-year-age drinking law revealed that only 6% intended to stop drinking, 70% planned to change their drinking location, 21% expected to use a false or borrowed identification to obtain alcohol and 22% intended to use other drugs. Anecdotal statements by students indicated the belief of some that it "might be easier to hide a little pot in my room than a six pack of beer."

Over the past four decades it has been demonstrated that the proportion of collegiate drinkers increases with age. However, in July of 1987, the minimum purchase age became 21 in all states. Because drinking tends to be highly valued among collegians and because it is now illegal for those under 21 to purchase alcohol, Dr. Ruth Engs and I hypothesized that reactance motivation would be stimulated among such students, leading more of them to drink. The data from 3,375 students at 56 colleges across the country revealed that, after the legislation, significantly more under-age students drank compared to those of legal age. Thus, the increase in purchase age appears to have been not only ineffective but actually counter-productive, at least in the short run.

The prohibitionists and their current neo-prohibitionists counterparts are clearly wrong in their assumptions. Drinking in moderation is neither undesirable nor dangerous but is actually associated with better health and greater longevity than is either abstention or heavy drinking. In short it is not bad but good and healthful. And drinking does not typically result in problem behavior. Similarly, moderate drinking is clearly not a forerunner of inebriation. To the contrary, the vast majority of drinkers enjoy the benefits of alcohol and never become problem drinkers.

People become responsible by being properly taught, given responsibility, and then held accountable for their actions. We don't tell young people to "just say no" to driving, fail to teach them to drive, and then on their 18th birthday give them driver's licenses and turn them loose on the road. But this is the logic we follow for beverage alcohol because neoprohibitionism underlies our alcohol policy.

It's time for our alcohol policy to be based on science rather than ideology.

Periodical Bibliography

The following articles have been selected to supplement the diverse views presented in this chapter.

Debra Baker — "Beer Battered Fans," *ABA Journal*, September 1999.

William F. Buckley Jr. — "More Political Correctness at Dartmouth," *Conservative Chronicle*, March 3, 1999.

Business Wire — "Drunken Driving Not Reduced by Higher Alcohol Taxes," January 3, 2000.

Bill Clinton — "President's Radio Address," *Weekly Compilation of Presidential Documents*, January 4, 1999.

Randy W. Elder et al. — ".08 BAC Laws Save Lives," December 10, 2001. www.washingtonpost.com.

Rudy Giuliani — "Should Vehicles Be Confiscated for Drunk Driving Offenses?: Yes," *Washington Post Weekly Edition*, December 13, 1999.

Enoch Gordis — "Research on Alcohol Problems," *National Forum*, Fall 1999.

Health and Medicine Week — "Program Seeks to Stop Problem Drinking in Children Ages 9–15," January 28, 2002.

Hans Nichols — "Getting Drunk on Rebellion," *Insight*, July 16, 2001.

David Pitt — "Higher Beer Taxes Would Reduce Gonorrhea," Associated Press, April 27, 2000. www.earthlink.net.

Anna Quindlen — "The Drug That Pretends It Isn't," *Newsweek*, April 10, 2000.

USA Today — "States Consider Raising Beer Taxes to Help Balance Budget," April 3, 2003.

U.S. Department of Health and Human Services — "10th Special Report to the U.S. Congress on Alcohol and Health," June 2000. www.os.dhhs.gov.

U.S. Department of Justice — "Costs of Underage Drinking," October 1999. www.usdoj.gov.

U.S. General Accounting Office — "Report to Congressional Committees: Effectiveness of State .08 Blood Alcohol Laws," June 1999. www.gao.gov.

Elizabeth Whelan — "Let Jenna and Barbara Have a Drink," American Council on Science and Health, June 6, 2001. www.acsh.org.

For Further Discussion

Chapter 1

1. Male health professionals (doctors, dentists, veterinarians) comprised the subjects observed in the Harvard School of Public Health study, which concluded that frequent, moderate drinking is beneficial. In contrast, the study that George Davey-Smith uses to support his argument that the benefits of frequent, moderate drinking have been exaggerated used middle-aged men from West Scotland as study subjects. Does the choice of study subjects affect the credibility of the authors' arguments? Explain.

2. Stanton Peele argues that patients should be told of the potential health benefits and risks of alcohol, which would allow them to choose for themselves whether or not to drink. Charlotte LoBuono maintains that since the health benefits of alcohol are not fully substantiated while the detrimental effects are well known, medical professionals should not encourage their patients to begin drinking. Which argument is more convincing? Explain, citing from the viewpoints.

3. Using a study by the National Center on Addiction and Substance Abuse at Columbia University (CASA) for support, Joseph A. Califano Jr. argues that underage drinking is a significant teen health problem. However, Doug Bandow claims that the CASA study is filled with inaccuracies causing the center to exaggerate the problem. In your opinion do Bandow's assertions undermine the credibility of Califano's argument? Explain.

Chapter 2

1. Editors from the National Institutes of Health argue that those who begin drinking alcohol before age fifteen are more likely to become alcohol abusers or alcoholics than those who begin drinking later in life. Dwight B. Heath contends that young people in Europe are taught to drink at an early age and are no more likely to develop an alcohol disorder than those who do not drink until they are twenty-one. Who do you think makes a stronger argument? Explain, citing from both texts.

2. NIAAA argues that alcoholism is a complex disorder influenced by genetic and environmental factors. Stanton Peele and Richard DeGrandpre maintain that disorders such as alcoholism have no genetic basis. What do you think the effect would be on the behavior of drinkers if scientists were able to identify conclusively the genes that affect alcoholism? Do you think people would drink more or less?

3. The Center on Alcohol Marketing and Youth argues that the alcohol beverage industry targets alcohol ads to an underage market. The International Center for Alcohol Policies claims that the industry is very careful to market only to adults. Do you think it is possible for an industry to effectively police its own advertising on a voluntary basis? Or do you think that tighter government controls on alcohol advertising would protect youth better? Explain.

Chapter 3

1. Jeffrey Hon argues that alcoholism, like asthma, diabetes, or high blood pressure, is a chronic disease. Edward A. Dreyfus, however, claims that alcoholism is a controllable behavior, not a disease. Which author's evaluation of the disease concept of alcoholism is more credible? Cite the viewpoints as you explain your answer.

2. Robby Werner uses an explanation of the Twelve Steps and other information provided by Alcoholics Anonymous to support his argument that AA is effective in helping alcoholics achieve sobriety. Charles Bufe uses statistics to bolster his argument that Alcoholics Anonymous is ineffective at helping alcoholics get sober. Whose argument is more persuasive? Explain.

3. Stanton Peele, Heather Ogilvie, and experts from Behavior Medical Associates argue in favor of treatment alternatives to twelve-step programs. Why are alternatives necessary in their opinion? In your view, which treatments seem most promising for the treatment of alcoholism?

Chapter 4

1. The National Highway Traffic Safety Administration (NHTSA) argues that with a blood alcohol concentration (BAC) of .08 percent, almost everyone's driving skills are impaired. Rick Berman contends that most people with a BAC of .08 are not impaired; in consequence, he argues against the .08 BAC law. The NHTSA is a government agency charged with preventing motor vehicle accidents while Rick Berman represents an organization devoted to selling alcoholic beverages. How do the author's credentials affect your evaluation of each argument? Explain.

2. Alexander C. Wagenaar and Traci L. Toomey maintain that the establishment of a minimum legal drinking age (MLDA) of twenty-one is the most effective way to reduce the problems associated with underage drinking. However, David J. Hanson, argues that a MLDA of twenty-one is based on prohibitionist ideology rather than on scientific facts and is ineffective. Which argument do you find more persuasive? Cite the viewpoints and use examples from your own experience to construct your answer.

Organizations to Contact

The editors have compiled the following list of organizations concerned with the issues debated in this book. The descriptions are derived from materials provided by the organizations. All have publications or information available for interested readers. The list was compiled on the date of publication of the present volume; names, addresses, phone and fax numbers, and e-mail and Internet addresses may change. Be aware that many organizations take several weeks or longer to respond to inquiries, so allow as much time as possible.

Al-Anon Family Group Headquarters
1600 Corporate Landing Pkwy., Virginia Beach, VA 23454
(757) 563-1600 • fax: (757) 563-1655
website: www.al/anon.alateen.org

Al-Anon is a fellowship of men, women, and children whose lives have been affected by an alcoholic family member or friend. Members share their experiences, strength, and hope to help each other and perhaps to aid in the recovery of the alcoholic. Al-Anon Family Group Headquarters provides information on its local chapters and on its affiliated organization, Alateen. Its publications include the monthly magazine the *Forum*, the semiannual *Al-Anon Speaks Out*, the bimonthly *Alateen Talk*, and several books, including *How Al-Anon Works, Path to Recovery: Steps, Traditions, and Concepts*, and *Courage to Be Me: Living with Alcoholism.*

Alcohol Advisory Council of New Zealand
Level 13, Castrol House, 36 Customhouse Quay, P.O. Box 5023, Wellington, New South Wales, New Zealand
04-472-0997 • fax: 04-473-0890
e-mail: central@alac.org.nz • website: www.alcohol.org.nz

The Alcohol Advisory Council of New Zealand's primary objective is to promote moderation in the use of alcohol and develop and promote strategies that will reduce alcohol problems for the nation. ALAC has a Maori Unit that coordinates culturally appropriate initiatives to reduce alcohol-related harm for the Maori. The organization publishes a quarterly newsletter in addition to research reports and government studies. All publications are available on the website.

Alcoholics Anonymous (AA)
General Service Office
PO Box 459, Grand Central Station, New York, NY 10163
(212) 870-3400 • fax: (212) 870-3003
website: www.aa.org

Alcoholics Anonymous is an international fellowship of people who are recovering from alcoholism. Because AA's primary goal is to help alcoholics remain sober, it does not sponsor research or engage in education about alcoholism. AA does, however, publish a catalog of literature concerning the organization as well as several pamphlets, including *Is AA for You? Young People and AA*, and *A Brief Guide to Alcoholics Anonymous.*

American Society of Addiction Medicine (ASAM)
4601 N. Park Ave., Upper Arcade No. 101, Chevy Chase, MD 20815
(301) 656-3920 • fax: (301) 656-3815
e-mail: email@asam.org • website: www.asam.org

ASAM is the nation's addiction medicine specialty society dedicated to educating physicians and improving the treatment of individuals suffering from alcoholism and other addictions. In addition, the organization promotes research and prevention of addiction and works for the establishment of addiction medicine as a specialty recognized by the American Board of Medical Specialties. The organization publishes medical texts and a bimonthly newsletter.

Canadian Centre on Substance Abuse/Centre canadien de lutte contre l'alcoolisme et les toxicomanies (CCSA/CCLAT)
75 Albert St., Suite 300, Ottawa, ON K1P 5E7 Canada
(800) 214-4788 • (613) 235-4048 • fax: (613) 235-8101
website: www.ccsa.ca

A Canadian clearinghouse on substance abuse, the CCSA/CCLAT works to disseminate information on the nature, extent, and consequences of substance abuse and to support and assist organizations involved in substance abuse treatment, prevention, and educational programming. The CCSA/CCLAT publishes several books, including *Canadian Profile: Alcohol, Tobacco, and Other Drugs*, as well as reports, policy documents, brochures, research papers, and the newsletter *Action News.*

Centre for Addiction and Mental Health/Centre de toxicomanie at de santé mentale (CAMH)
33 Russell St., Toronto, ON M5S 2S1 Canada
(416) 535-8501 • toll free: (800) 463-6273
website: www.camh.net

CAMH is a public hospital and the largest addiction facility in Canada. It also functions as a research facility, an education and training center, and a community-based organization providing health and addiction prevention services throughout Ontario, Canada. Further, CAMH is a Pan American Health Organization and World Health Organization Collaborating Centre. CAMH publishes the quarterly *CrossCurrents*, the *Journal of Addiction and Mental Health* and offers free alcoholism prevention literature that can either be downloaded or ordered on the website.

Distilled Spirits Council of the United States (DISCUS)
1250 I St. NW, Suite 900, Washington, DC 20005
(202) 628-3544
website: www.discus.org

The Distilled Spirits Council of the United States is the national trade association representing producers and marketers of distilled spirits in the United States. It seeks to ensure the responsible advertising and marketing of distilled spirits to adult consumers and to prevent such advertising and marketing from targeting individuals below the legal purchase age. DISCUS publishes fact sheets, the periodic newsletter *News Release*, and several pamphlets, including the *Drunk Driving Prevention Act*.

International Center for Alcohol Policies (ICAP)
1519 New Hampshire Ave. NW, Washington, DC 20036
(202) 986-1159 • fax: (202) 986-2080
website: www.icap.org

The International Center for Alcohol Policies is a nonprofit organization dedicated to helping reduce the abuse of alcohol worldwide and to promote understanding of the role of alcohol in society through dialogue and partnerships involving the beverage industry, the public health community, and others interested in alcohol policy. ICAP is supported by eleven major international beverage alcohol companies. ICAP publishes reports on pertinent issues such as *Safe Alcohol Consumption*, *The Limits of Binge Drinking*, *Health Warning Labels*, *Drinking Age Limits*, *What Is a "Standard Drink"?*, *Government Policies on Alcohol and Pregnancy*, *Estimating Costs Associated with Alcohol Abuse*, and *Who Are the Abstainers?*

Mothers Against Drunk Driving (MADD)
511 E. John Carpenter Fwy., No. 700, Irving, TX 75062
(800) GET-MADD • fax: (972) 869-2206
e-mail: info@madd.org • website: www.madd.org

Mothers Against Drunk Driving seeks to act as the voice of victims of drunk driving accidents by speaking on their behalf to communities, businesses, and educational groups, and by providing materials for use in medical facilities and health and driver education programs. MADD publishes the biannual *MADDvocate for Victims Magazine* and the newsletter *MADD in Action* as well as a variety of brochures and other materials on drunk driving.

National Council on Alcoholism and Drug Dependence (NCADD)
12 W. 21st St., New York, NY 10010
(212) 206-6770 • fax: (212) 645-1690
website: www.ncadd.org

NCADD is a volunteer health organization that helps individuals overcome addictions, advises the federal government on drug and alcohol policies, and develops substance abuse prevention and education programs for youth. It publishes fact sheets, such as *Youth and Alcohol*, and pamphlets, such as *Who's Got the Power? You . . . or Drugs?*

National Institute on Alcoholism and Alcohol Abuse (NIAAA)
6000 Executive Blvd., Wilco Building, Bethesda, MD 20892-7003
website: www.niaaa.nih.gov

The National Institute on Alcoholism and Alcohol Abuse is one of the eighteen institutes that comprise the National Institutes of Health. NIAAA provides leadership in the national effort to reduce alcohol-related problems. NIAAA is an excellent source of information and publishes the quarterly bulletin, *Alcohol Alert;* a quarterly scientific journal, *Alcohol Research and Health;* and many pamphlets, brochures, and posters dealing with alcohol abuse and alcoholism. All of these publications, including NIAAA's congressional testimony, are available online.

National Organization on Fetal Alcohol Syndrome (NOFAS)
216 G St. NE, Washington, DC 20002
(202) 785-4585 • (800) 66 NOFAS • fax: (202) 466-6456
e-mail: information@nofas.org • website: www.nofas.org

NOFAS is a nonprofit organization dedicated to eliminating birth defects caused by alcohol consumption during pregnancy and improving the quality of life for those individuals and families affected. The organization sponsors many outreach and educational programs and publishes a quarterly newsletter, *Notes from NOFAS*, in addition to many fact sheets and brochures. Some information is available online. An information packet can be ordered through the mail.

Office for Substance Abuse Prevention (OSAP)
National Clearinghouse for Alcohol and Drug Information (NCADI)
PO Box 2345, Rockville, MD 20847-2345
(800) 729-6686 • TDD: (800) 487-4889
or (301) 230-2867 • (301) 468-2600
website: www.health.org

OSAP leads U.S. government efforts to prevent alcoholism and other drug problems among Americans. Through the NCADI, OSAP provides the public with a wide variety of information on alcoholism and other addictions. Its publications include the bimonthly *Prevention Pipeline*, the fact sheet *Alcohol Alert*, monographs such as "Social Marketing/Media Advocacy" and "Advertising and Alcohol," brochures, pamphlets, videotapes, and posters. Publications in Spanish are also available.

Rational Recovery Systems (RRS)
PO Box 800, Lotus, CA 95651
(916) 621-4374 • (800) 303-CURE • fax: (916) 621-2667
e-mail: rrsn@rational.org • website: www.rational.org/recovery

RRS is a national self-help organization that offers a cognitive rather than spiritual approach to recovery from alcoholism. Its philosophy holds that alcoholics can attain sobriety without depending on other people or a "higher power." Rational Recovery Systems publishes materials about the organization and its use of rational-emotive therapy.

Research Society on Alcoholism (RSA)
4314 Medical Pkwy., Suite 12, Austin, TX 78756
(512) 454-0022 • fax: (512) 454-0812
e-mail: debbyrsa@bga.com • website: www.rsoa.org

The RSA provides a forum for researchers who share common interests in alcoholism. The society's purpose is to promote research on the prevention and treatment of alcoholism. It publishes the journal *Alcoholism: Clinical and Experimental Research* nine times a year as well as the book series Recent Advances in Alcoholism.

Secular Organizations for Sobriety (SOS)
PO Box 5, Buffalo, NY 14215
(716) 834-2922
website: www.secularsobriety.org

SOS is a network of groups dedicated to helping individuals achieve and maintain sobriety. The organization believes that alcoholics can best recover by rationally choosing to make sobriety rather than alcohol a priority. Most members of SOS reject the spiritual basis of Alcoholics Anonymous and other similar self-help groups. SOS publishes the quarterly *SOS International Newsletter* and distributes the books *Unhooked: Staying Sober and Drug Free* and *How to Stay Sober: Recovery Without Religion*, written by SOS founder James Christopher.

Bibliography of Books

Alcoholics Anonymous World Service — *Alcoholics Anonymous.* New York: Alcoholics Anonymous World Service, 2000.

American Health Research Institute — *Fetal Alcohol Syndrome—The Man-Made Disease for Babies and Children: Index of New Information.* Washington, DC: ABBE Publishers Association of Washington, DC, 1999.

Anatoly Antoshechkin — *Alcohol: Poison or Medicine?* Bloomington, IN: 1st Books Library, 2002.

Charles Bufe — *Alcoholics Anonymous: Cult or Cure?* Tucson, AZ: See Sharp Press, 1998.

Rosalyn Carson-Dewitt, ed. — *Encyclopedia of Drugs, Alcohol, and Addictive Behavior.* New York: MacMillan Library Reference, 2001.

Carol Colleran and Debra Erickson Jay — *Aging and Addiction: Helping Older Adults Overcome Alcohol or Medication Dependence.* Center City, MN: Hazelden Information Education, 2002.

Griffiths Edwards — *Alcohol: The World's Favorite Drug.* New York: Thomas Dunne Books, 2002.

Kathleen Whelen Fitzgerald — *Alcoholism: The Genetic Inheritance.* Friday Harbor, WA: Whales Tales Press, 2002.

Anne M. Fletcher — *Sober for Good.* Boston: Houghton Mifflin, 2001.

Gene Ford — *The Science of Healthy Drinking.* San Francisco: Wine Appreciation Guild, 2003.

Judith Goodman — *The Female Alcoholic.* Temecula, CA: Women and Addiction Counseling and Educational Services, 2000.

Raymond V. Haring — *Shattering Myths and Mysteries of Alcohol: Insights and Answers to Drinking, Smoking, and Drug Use.* Sacramento: Healthspan Communications, 1998.

Dwight B. Heath — *Drinking Occasions: Comparative Perspectives on Alcohol and Culture.* New York: Brunner-Routledge, 2000.

John Jung — *Psychology of Alcohol and Other Drugs: A Research Perspective.* Thousand Oaks, CA: Sage, 2000.

Katherine Ketchum et al. — *Under the Influence: Understanding and Defeating Alcoholism.* New York: Bantam Dell, 2000.

Jodee Kulp — *The Best I Can Be: Living with Fetal Alcohol Syndrome.* St. Paul, MN: Better Endings, New Beginnings, 2000.

Gene Logsdon and Michael Jackson — *Good Spirits: A New Look at Ol' Demon Alcohol.* White River Junction, VT: Chelsea Green, 1999.

Eric Newhouse — *Alcohol: Cradle to Grave.* Center City, MN: Hazelden Information Education, 2001.

Thomas Nordegren — *The A–Z Encyclopedia of Alcohol and Drug Abuse.* Parkland, FL: Brown Walker Press, 2002.

Heather Ogilvie et al. — *Alternatives to Abstinence: A New Look at Alcoholism and Choices in Treatment.* Long Island City, NY: Hatherleigh Press, 2001.

Nancy Olson — *With a Lot of Help from Our Friends: The Politics of Alcoholism.* New York: Writers Club Press, 2003.

Stanton Peele — *The Meaning of Addiction: An Unconventional View.* San Francisco: Jossey-Bass, 1998.

Thomas R. Pegram — *Battling Demon Rum: The Struggle for a Dry America, 1800–1933.* Chicago: Ivan R. Dee, 1999.

J. Vincent Peterson et al. — *A Nation Under the Influence: America's Addiction to Alcohol.* Boston: Allyn and Bacon, 2002.

Bert Pluymen — *The Thinking Person's Guide to Sobriety.* New York: Griffin Trade Paperback, 2000.

Susan Powter — *Sober . . . and Staying That Way: The Missing Link in the Cure for Alcoholism.* New York: Fireside, 1999.

Frederick Rotgers et al. — *Responsible Drinking: A Moderation Management Approach for Problem Drinkers.* Oakland, CA: New Harbinger, 2002.

Lori Rotskoff — *Love on the Rocks: Men, Women, and Alcohol in Post–World War II America.* Chapel Hill: University of North Carolina Press, 2002.

Joseph Santoro et al. — *Kill the Craving: How to Control the Impulse to Use Drugs and Alcohol.* Oakland, CA: New Harbinger, 2001.

Marc Alan Schuckit — *Educating Yourself About Alcohol and Drugs: A People's Primer.* Cambridge, MA: HarperCollins Publishers, 1998.

Frank A. Sloan and Emily M. Stout, eds. — *Drinkers, Drivers, and Bartenders: Balancing Private Choices and Public Accountability.* Chicago: University of Chicago Press, 2000.

James P. Spradley — *You Owe Yourself a Drunk: An Ethnography of Urban Nomads.* Prospect Heights, IL: Waveland Press, 1999.

Joseph Volpicelli and Maja Szalavitz	*Recovery Options: The Complete Guide.* New York: John Wiley and Sons, 2000.
Ronald R. Watson and Adam K. Myers, eds.	*Alcohol and Heart Disease.* London: Taylor and Francis, 2002.
Henry Wechsler and Bernice Wuethrich	*Dying to Drink: Confronting Binge Drinking on College Campuses.* Emmaus, PA: Rodale Press, 2002.
Danny M. Wilcox	*Alcoholic Thinking.* Westport, CT: Praeger, 1998.

Index

National Council on Alcoholism and Drug Dependence, 100
National Highway Traffic Safety Administration (NHTSA), 54, 157, 164
National Household Survey on Drug Abuse, 45
National Institute on Alcohol Abuse and Alcoholism (NIAAA), 50, 53, 56, 60
National Institutes of Health, 52
National Longitudinal Alcohol Epidemiologic Survey (NLAES), 53
National Organization of Fetal Alcohol Syndrome (NOFAS), 10
Native Americans, 67
Nery, Jason, 57
New England Journal of Medicine, 18, 142, 165
New York Times (newspaper), 163
Ninth Special Report to the U.S. Congress on Alcohol Abuse and Alcoholism (NIAAA), 50, 61
Noble, Ernest, 73–74
nondrinkers. *See* abstinence/abstainers

obesity, 75
Ogilvie, Heather, 130
Orthodox Jews, 56

parents, 90
Peele, Stanton, 26, 70, 137–38, 139
peer influence, 90
personal responsibility
    alcoholics can control drinking, 133
    behavioral changes are required for recovery, 99–100
    exists in all, 74–75
    is denied by
        Alcoholics Anonymous, 116–17, 118
        disease model, 105, 109–10, 137–38
    genetic factors as cause of, 71–72
    learned helplessness and, 78–79
    treatments based on, 95–96, 141
pharmaceuticals. *See* medications
physical injury, 34
Pinel, Phillippe, 106
platelet function, 19–20
polyphenols, 16
pregnancy, 10–12
Prescott, Katherine, 163
problem drinking. *See* abuse
prohibitionism, 30–31, 57, 58, 172

Quarterly Journal of Studies on Alcohol, 121

race, 37, 61–62, 67, 68
Radio National, 21
Raphael, Rebecca, 135
Rational Behavior Therapy, 128–29
Rational Recovery, 95–96
religion, 117–18, 119, 127, 137
Renaud, Serge, 15
Report to Congress (NHTSA), 161
Revia (naltrexone), 143, 151
Rimm, Eric, 20
Room, Robin, 123
Ross, H. Laurence, 156
Rush, Benjamin, 100, 105
Russia, 24

Schuckit, Marc, 50
Scotland, study in, 22–25
Secular Organizations for Sobriety, 144
self-efficacy. *See* personal responsibility
Seligman, Martin, 78
sexual behavior, 40, 84–85
Shalala, Donna, 46, 53
60 Minutes (TV series), 15
Smerber v. California, 160
Sobell, Linda, 134
Sobell, Mark, 134
social classes
    alcoholism and, 76–77
    patterns of consumption and, 23
spirits
    binge drinking of, 31
    television advertising of, 82, 84, 91
spontaneous remissions, 125–26, 132, 136
statin drugs, 27
strokes and consumption, 22–24, 25, 34
Study of Adult Development (Harvard Medical School), 132–33
Substance Abuse and Mental Health Services Administration, 45
Supreme Court, 160
Szasz, Thomas, 105

teenagers. *See* underage drinking/drinkers
television advertising
    is effective, 86
    is misleading, 81, 84
    underage drinkers and
        exposure to, is significant, 42, 81–84, 86
        impact on
            is minimal, 90, 92
            is negative, 84–85
    voluntary industry guidelines for, 82, 85, 90

191